THE RUM 1000

The Ultimate Collection of Rum Cocktails, Recipes, Facts, and Resources

Ray Foley

SOURCEBOOKS, INC.
NAPERVILLE, ILLINOIS

Published by Sourcebooks, Inc.
P.O. Box 4410, Naperville, Illinois 60567-4410
(630) 961-3900
Fax: (630) 961-2168
www.sourcebooks.com

Library of Congress Cataloging-in-Publication Data

Foley, Ray.
 The rum 1000 : the ultimate collection of rum cocktails, recipes, facts, and resources / Ray Foley.
    p. cm.
 Includes index.
 1. Cocktails. 2. Rum. 3. Cookery (Rum) I. Title. II. Title: Rum one thousand. III. Title: Rum thousand.

TX951.F59457 2008
641.8'74—dc22
                              2007051445

Printed and bound in the United States of America.

BG 10 9 8 7 6 5 4 3 2 1

DEDICATION

To:
Jaclyn Marie Foley and Ryan

plus

The Other Tribe: Raymond Pindar, Amy, and Mr. Bill

also

The Readers of *Bartender Magazine,*
www.bartender.com, and www.USBartender.com

CONTENTS

ACKNOWLEDGMENTS

First and foremost, Sara Kase and Peter Lynch at Sourcebooks (www.sourcebooks.com).

I would also like to thank the following for their assistance in the completion of this book:

Vic Morrison at McCormick Distilling; Greg Cohen at the Richards Group in Dallas; Pyrat Rum; Michel Roux at Crillon Importers; Jim Nikola at Crillon Importers; the great folks at Bacardi; Jose Cuervo; Diageo; Tabasco; the Food Group; Skyy Spirits; Barton Brands; Cointreau; Coco Lopez; Lyndon Chin at Group LIH; Rums of Puerto Rico; Henry Preiss at PreissImports.com; Larrain Gracia at Edelman.com; Tortuga Rum Company; Angostura, Ltd.; Pusser Rum; Cruzan Rum; Laura Baddish at the Baddish Group; Sarah Zeller of Sidney Frank Importing Co.; Michael Kuropatkin of Carat, N.Y.C.; Jeff Pogash at Moët Hennessy; Peter Nelson and crew at Niche Importing, New Jersey; and all the other rum companies that assisted in the completion of *The Rum 1000*.

To Marc Pickard for keeping my computer going; Erin Mackey for her assistance, being the best, and continuing her education; Loretta Natiello for being my best friend; Jimmy Zazzali, for being a great bartender and friend; Matt Wojciak; John Cowan; Mike Cammarano; Marvin Solomon; Jack Foley, Jr.; and, of course, the great Hymie Lipshitz.

And also to all those who submitted recipes to www.bartender.com and the readers of *Bartender Magazine*.

To all the great bartenders who have served me in America and around the world!

The Best!

INTRODUCTION

Yo! Ho! Ho! And a bottle of rum!

From history to recipes to resources, *The Rum 1000* will assist you in the drinking and cooking of rum like no other book will.

Whether you are a home bartender or a professional bartender, this guide will be a great reference. Keep it next to your bottle of rum.

A few notes on the recipes:

Sugar-free juice or diet soda can be substituted in any drink. For example, if a recipe calls for lemonade, feel free to use sugar-free lemonade; if a recipe calls for tonic, feel free to use diet tonic.

For martinis containing vermouth, the less vermouth, the drier the martini.

Enjoy! Please drink in moderation and NEVER drink and drive. If you have any questions, I can be reached at barmag@aol.com.

For more information on bartending, go to www.bartender.com.

75 RUM FACTS

The origins of rum date back more than two thousand years.
The origin of sugarcane is Papua, New Guinea.
Christopher Columbus first brought sugarcane to the Caribbean.
Ponce de Leon planted the first sugarcane fields in Puerto Rico.
The first sugar mill was built in Puerto Rico in 1525.
The first still was built in 1893.
The first rum was exported to the United States in 1897.
The first rum distillery in the United States appeared in 1664.
Rum was used as a cure-all for many ailments in the Caribbean.

"Rum" is from the word *rumbullion*.
Rumbullion means "a great tumult or uproar."
Others claim "rum" is from the Dutch word *roemer*.
Roemer means "a drinking glass."

Other names used for rum are: Nelson Blood,
    Navy Neater,
    Demon Water, and
    Pirate's Drink.

Rum is made from sugarcane by-products.
Sugarcane's by-products are molasses and sugarcane juice.

Crude rum is first distilled to between 125 and 180 proof.

Most, but not all, rums come from Puerto Rico and the West Indies.
Other countries producing rum are Brazil (called *cachaca*),
   Venezuela,
   the United States,
   Canada (known as *Screech*),
   Australia,
   Cuba,
   Bermuda (Gosling's), and
   Africa.

Rum also served as a medium of exchange and barter.
Don Facundo Bacardi Masso is responsible for experimenting with
   distillation techniques; he is thus responsible for modern light rums
   and Bacardi.
Bacardi Y Compania was founded in 1862.
Today Bacardi is the number one rum in the world.
Puerto Rico is the largest producer of rum.

There are seven types, or grades, of rum.
Light rums are also called:
   White or
   Silver.
   Gold rums are also called amber.
   Spiced rums are flavored by adding spices and sometimes caramel.
   Dark rum is also known as black rum.

There are many types of flavored rums, such as coconut,
   Orange,
   Mango, and
   Citron.

Premium rums are made from small batches of aged and gently
   distilled rum.

Overproof rums are rums with an alcohol percentage higher than 40, or rums higher than 80 proof.

A cream rum, or cream-produced rum, is Cruzan 34, but this is not a type or grade.

Most rum is aged for at least one year.
Some rums are aged in used bourbon casks.
Some rums are aged in other types of wooden casks.
Other rums are aged in stainless steel tanks.
Because of the tropical climate, rum matures faster than other types of alcohol.

As much as 10 percent of rum is lost during aging through evaporation.
This is called "the angel's share."
After aging, rum is blended to ensure great flavor.

Rhum is a term used in French-speaking islands.
Ron Añejo means a rum that has been significantly aged.
Rhums, or agricultural Rhums, are distilled directly from harvested sugarcane.

In 2006, 22.7 million cases of rum were sold in the U.S.
Puerto Rican rum distillers sell about 70 percent of all rum in the United States.

The British Royal Navy gave its sailors a daily rum ration until July 31, 1970.
This ration was known as a "tot."

Cachaca is similar to rum, but it is triple distilled and produced in Brazil.

Rupert Holmes's song "Escape (the Piña Colada Song)" was a popular rum song.
Paul Revere ordered a mug of rum before his famous ride.

Ben Franklin invented the Rum Flip.
Rum could have been in the very first mixed cocktail.

George Washington had a barrel of Barbados rum at his 1789 inauguration.

Mojitos are the new popular rum cocktail. (Be sure to try the great recipes included in this book! See pages 162–173.)
Cuba Libre (rum, Coke, and a lime wedge) means "Free Cuba."
Rum and coke is one of the world's most popular cocktails.

Rum is also used in a number of food dishes.
Bananas Foster (see page 256) is a very popular dish made with rum.
Today rum gives vodka competition as the number one mixer.

700 RUM COCKTAILS

267 SUNDOWNER

1 oz. 267 Infusion mango rum
1 oz. 267 Infusion pineapple rum
mint sprig for garnish

Serve on the rocks. Garnish with a fresh mint sprig.

267 SWEET ESCAPE

1 part 267 Infusion mango rum
1 part 267 Infusion cranberry vodka

Keep it simple but sweet with or without a garnish.

3 O'CLOCK SKIPPER POOL COCKTAIL

2 oz. 10 Cane rum
1 oz. simple syrup
1½ oz. fresh-squeezed lemon juice (from about 1 lemon)
3–4 mint leaves (bruise dry leaves with a muddler in a shaker)
splash 7UP or Sprite
mint sprig for garnish
lemon wheel for garnish

In a mixing glass, combine 10 Cane, simple syrup, lemon juice, and mint leaves. Add ice and shake vigorously. Strain and pour into a rocks glass. Top with 7UP or Sprite. Garnish with mint sprig and lemon wheel.

40C'S MALIBU BLUE PARADISE RUM

½ part Malibu coconut rum
½ part blue curacao
½ part peach schnapps
¼ part sweet and sour mix
dash lemon-lime soda

Developed by 40C, New York.

ADMIRAL'S QUENCHER

1½ oz. Admiral Nelson's premium coconut rum
1 oz. Arrow melon liqueur
2 oz. orange juice
2 oz. pineapple juice
orange slice for garnish

Serve over ice. Garnish with orange slice.

ADULT FILM STARR

2 oz. Starr African rum
½ oz. Licor 43
1 oz. lime juice
¼ oz. simple syrup
3 cucumber slices (plus more for garnish)
ground cinnamon
ground nutmeg

Muddle cucumber slices in a rocks glass. Add all other ingredients and mix well, then place crushed ice on top. Garnish with grated nutmeg, cinnamon, and cucumber slices.

AFTER CARNIVAL DRINK

1 oz. white Barbancourt rum
½ oz. gin
½ oz. sambuca
1 oz. orange juice
½ oz. lemon-lime soda
½ oz. simple syrup
1 kiwi slice

Shake with ice and strain into a highball glass filled with ice cubes.

AFTERBURNER

2 oz. Wray & Nephew rum
½ oz. peppermint schnapps
½ oz. Kahlúa

Pour ingredients into a snifter glass. Swirl to mix.

ALI-COLADA

dash Bacardi rum
2 oz. Alizé liqueur
2 oz. Coco Lopez real cream of coconut
pineapple wedge for garnish

Blend. Garnish with pineapple wedge.

ALNWICK'S 43

½ oz. Alnwick rum
dash orange juice
dash crème de cassis

Shake and pour into a shot glass.

ALOHA

1 oz. dark rum
½ oz. fresh lime juice
2 oz. pineapple juice
2 oz. fresh orange juice
1 oz. Coco Lopez real cream of coconut
small scoop vanilla ice cream
pineapple spear for garnish
maraschino cherry for garnish

Blend. Garnish with pineapple spear and maraschino cherry.

ALPINE GLOW

1 oz. Gosling's Black Seal rum (plus ½ oz. to float)
½ oz. brandy
½ oz. triple sec
2 oz. sweet and sour mix
splash grenadine
lemon twist for garnish

Shake first four ingredients over ice and serve on the rocks. Float ½ oz. Gosling's Black Seal rum and garnish with lemon twist.

ANGOSTURA FUH SO

1 oz. Angostura white rum
1 oz. amaretto
1 oz. heavy cream
fresh cinnamon to taste
3–4 dashes Angostura aromatic bitters
½ oz. grenadine

Blend first five ingredients and layer on grenadine.

ANGOSTURA ROYALE

2 oz. Angostura 1919 premium rum
1 oz. Cointreau
½ oz. blue curaçao
2 oz. pineapple juice
3–4 dashes Angostura aromatic bitters
lime wedges for garnish

Shake and garnish with lime wedges.

ANGOSTURA STINGER

1 oz. Angostura 1919 premium rum
½ oz. white crème de cacao
¼ oz. white crème de menthe
1 oz. heavy cream
dash blue food coloring
3–4 dashes Angostura aromatic bitters
cherries for garnish
parsley for garnish

Shake and garnish with cherries and parsley snips.

APPLE DAIQUIRI

1 oz. light rum
1 oz. apple schnapps
½ oz. sweet and sour mix
¼ apple, peeled
apple slice for garnish

Blend. Garnish with apple slice.

APPLE PIE À LA MODE

¾ oz. Captain Morgan original spiced rum
½ oz. apple schnapps
2 oz. apple juice
2 tbsp. apple pie filling
1 oz. cream of coconut
1 oz. heavy cream
16-oz. scoop crushed ice
cinnamon for sprinkling
apple wedge or cinnamon stick for garnish

Blend until smooth and creamy. Serve in specialty glass. Garnish with apple wedge or cinnamon stick.

APPLESAUCE

1 oz. Captain Morgan original spiced rum
3 oz. applesauce
4 oz. sweet and sour mix/margarita mix
¼ oz. triple sec

Blend with 12 oz. ice until slushy. Serve in a 15-oz. glass.

APPLETON BLUE LAGOON

1½ oz. Appleton Estate V/X Jamaica rum
1 oz. blue curaçao
5 oz. lemonade
lime wedge for garnish

Pour into a highball or Collins glass over ice and stir. Garnish with lime wedge.

APPLETON BOSSA NOVA

1½ oz. Appleton Estate V/X rum
¼ oz. lime juice
¼ oz. lemon juice
5 oz. passion fruit juice
orange slice for garnish

Combine in a shaker and mix well. Serve in a colada glass over ice. Garnish with orange slice.

APPLETON CARIBBEAN COSMO

1½ oz. Appleton Estate V/X Jamaica rum
¾ oz. triple sec
splash lime juice
cranberry juice to taste

Mix well and pour into a rocks glass over ice.

APPLETON CARIBBEAN SEA

1½ oz. Appleton Estate V/X Jamaica rum
¾ oz. blue curacao
3 oz. pineapple juice
1½ oz. coconut cream
pineapple wedge for garnish
cherry for garnish

Blend with ice. Serve in a cocktail or margarita glass and garnish with pineapple wedge and cherry.

APPLETON COSMO ENCOUNTER

1½ oz. Appleton Estate V/X Jamaica rum
½ oz. triple sec
splash lime juice
cranberry juice to taste
lime twist for garnish

Mix well and serve in a martini glass. Garnish with a twist of lime.

APPLETON DOCTOR BIRD

1½ oz. Appleton Estate V/X Jamaica rum
3 oz. pineapple juice
1 tsp. sugar
½ lime
3 oz. ginger ale
pineapple wedge for garnish
cherry for garnish

Cut up the lime. Blend with first three ingredients and mix until smooth. Pour into a Collins or rocks glass, top with ginger ale, and garnish with pineapple wedge and cherry.

APPLETON ELUSIVE REDHEAD

1½ oz. Appleton Estate V/X Jamaica rum
3 oz. Clamato or Bloody Mary mix
horseradish to taste
Tabasco to taste
sea salt to taste, plus more to rim glass
black pepper to taste, plus more to rim glass
Worcestershire sauce to taste
lime juice to taste
celery stick for garnish
olives for garnish
Tomolives for garnish

*Season to taste with horseradish, Tabasco, pepper, sea salt, Worcester-
shire sauce, and lime juice. Rim glass in sea salt and/or pepper. Pour
into glass. Garnish with a celery stick, olives, and Tomolives.*

APPLETON ESTATE V/X AND SODA/TONIC

2 oz. Appleton Estate V/X Jamaica rum
½ oz. sherry
drizzle of sweet vermouth
maraschino cherry for garnish

*Pour rum into a rocks glass over ice, add sherry and sweet vermouth,
and garnish with maraschino cherry.*

APPLETON ESTATE V/X CLASSIC BANANA DAIQUIRI

2 oz. Appleton Estate V/X Jamaica rum
½ oz. fresh lime juice
1 oz. banana liqueur
¼ oz. simple syrup
lime slice for garnish

Shake with ice and strain into a martini glass. Garnish with a lime slice.

APPLETON ESTATE V/X CLASSIC MAI TAI

1 oz. Appleton Estate V/X Jamaica rum
1 oz. Appleton Estate Reserve Jamaica rum
½ oz. apricot brandy
½ oz. orange curaçao
dash grenadine
dash orgeat syrup
3 oz. fresh pineapple juice
½ oz. dark Coruba Jamaica rum (optional)
mint sprig for garnish

Shake with ice until foamy and pour into a Collins glass. Float dark Coruba Jamaica rum on top and garnish with a mint sprig.

APPLETON ESTATE V/X COSMOPOLITAN

1½ oz. Appleton Estate V/X Jamaica rum
½ oz. triple sec
splash lime juice
cranberry juice to taste
lime twist for garnish

Shake with ice and strain into a martini glass. Garnish with a twist of lime.

APPLETON ESTATE V/X HURRICANE

1½ oz. Appleton Estate V/X Jamaica rum
1½ oz. Coruba dark rum
splash Rose's lime juice
¼ oz. simple syrup
2 oz. fresh orange juice
2 oz. fresh pineapple juice
orange wheel for garnish
lime zest for garnish
lemon zest for garnish

Mix well and strain into a hurricane glass. Garnish with an orange wheel, lime zest, and lemon zest.

APPLETON ESTATE V/X MANHATTAN

2 oz. Appleton Estate V/X Jamaica rum
4 oz. soda
lime or lemon wedge for garnish

Pour into a rocks glass over ice. Garnish with a fresh lime or lemon wedge.

APPLETON ESTATE V/X PLANTER'S PUNCH

1½ oz. Appleton Estate V/X Jamaica rum
½ oz. grenadine
2 dashes Angostura bitters
1½ oz. sweet and sour mix
1½ oz. orange juice
orange wedge for garnish
cherry for garnish

Build in a tall glass over ice and stir. Garnish with orange wedge and cherry.

APPLETON EXOTIC LADY

1½ oz. Appleton Estate V/X Jamaica rum
2 oz. pineapple juice
2 oz. ginger ale
¼ oz. grenadine
½ lime
1 tsp. sugar
pineapple wedge for garnish
cherry for garnish

Cut up lime and mix with pineapple juice, rum, sugar, and grenadine over ice. Strain into a martini glass and top with ginger ale. Garnish with pineapple wedge and cherry.

APPLETON EXQUISITE DAIQUIRI

2 oz. Appleton Estate V/X Jamaica rum
½ oz. fresh lime juice
¼ oz. simple syrup
lime slice for garnish

Shake with ice and strain into a martini glass. Garnish with lime slice.

APPLETON GREEN PARROT

1½ oz. Appleton Estate V/X Jamaica rum
4 oz. orange juice
1 oz. blue curacao
orange slice for garnish

Pour ingredients one at a time in the order listed above into a stemware glass over ice. Do not mix. Garnish with orange slice.

APPLETON ISLAND ENTICEMENT

1 oz. Appleton Estate V/X Jamaica rum
1 oz. Midori melon liqueur
3 oz. pineapple juice
splash grenadine
pineapple wedge for garnish
cherry for garnish

Stir first three ingredients with ice. Pour into a glass, then float grenadine on top. Garnish with pineapple wedge and cherry.

APPLETON JAMAICA SUNSET

1½ oz. Appleton Estate V/X Jamaica rum
2½ oz. cranberry juice
3½ oz. orange juice
orange wheel for garnish

Pour first two ingredients into a highball or stemware glass over ice. Slowly add orange juice. Garnish with orange wheel.

APPLETON JAMAICAN ECSTASY DREAM

½ oz. Appleton Estate V/X Jamaica rum
½ oz. cranberry juice
½ oz. grapefruit juice
½ oz. orange juice
½ oz. club soda
orange wedge for garnish

In a highball glass, pour rum, cranberry juice, and grapefruit juice over ice. Slowly add orange juice and top with club soda. Garnish with orange wedge.

APPLETON JAMAICAN MARTINI

3 oz. Appleton Estate V/X Jamaica rum
1½ oz. lime juice
½ tsp. grenadine or strawberry syrup
lime wedge for garnish

Spoon grenadine into a chilled cocktail glass. Stir rum and lime over ice in a separate mixing glass and strain into the cocktail glass. Garnish with lime wedge.

APPLETON PURPLE DEW

1½ oz. Appleton Estate V/X Jamaica rum
3 oz. cranberry juice
1 oz. clear syrup
1 oz. blue curaçao
1 oz. lime juice
pineapple wedge for garnish
cherry for garnish

Stir in a Collins or punch glass over ice. Garnish with pineapple wedge and cherry.

APPLETON YELLOW BIRD

1½ oz. Appleton Estate V/X Jamaica rum
3 oz. pineapple juice
½ oz. orange juice
¾ oz. crème de banana
½ oz. apricot brandy
orange slice for garnish

Mix well. Strain into a Collins glass over ice and garnish with orange slice.

APRICOT PIÑA

1½ oz. light rum
½ oz. apricot brandy
1½ oz. unsweetened pineapple juice
1 oz. Coco Lopez real cream of coconut

Blend.

ARCHANGEL

2 oz. Wray & Nephew rum
¼ oz. strawberry puree
½ oz. peach schnapps
½ oz. cachaca
½ oz. pineapple juice
4 basil leaves for garnish

Shake with ice and strain into a Collins glass over ice. Garnish with basil leaves.

ARIANA'S DREAM

½ oz. Bacardi rum
1 oz. Alizé liqueur
1 oz. crème de cacao
3 oz. orange juice
fresh strawberry for garnish

Garnish with fresh strawberry.

ASSAM CHAI PUNCH

1½ oz. Pyrat XO Reserve rum
½ oz. Grand Marnier
1 oz. orange juice
1 oz. fresh sweet and sour
3 oz. chai tea
orange twist for garnish
mint sprig for garnish

Shake and strain over ice. Garnish with orange twist and fresh mint sprig.

BACARDI AMBER DAIQUIRI

2 oz. Bacardi dark rum
2 tsp. fresh lime or lemon juice
½ tsp. sugar
½ tsp. cream
grated nutmeg for garnish

Blend and serve in a tall glass. Garnish with nutmeg.

BACARDI ANCIENT MARINER

Equal parts:
   Bacardi Gold Reserve rum
   Grand Marnier

Stir with ice. Serve straight up or in a martini glass.

BACARDI BANANA COLADA

1½ oz. Bacardi light or dark rum
1 oz. Coco Lopez real cream of coconut
½ ripe banana

Blend with ½ cup ice or shake and serve on ice.

BACARDI BIG APPLE

1½ oz. Bacardi light or dark rum
¾ oz. lemon or lime juice
½ oz. apple brandy
¾ oz. grenadine
apple slice for garnish

Shake with ice and serve in a tall glass with ice. Garnish with apple slice.

BACARDI BLACK DIRTY COLADA

1¼ oz. Bacardi black rum
1 oz. Coco Lopez real cream of coconut
2 oz. pineapple juice

Blend.

BACARDI BLACK RUSSIAN

1 part coffee liqueur
2 parts Bacardi light rum

Stir over ice in a rocks glass.

BACARDI BLOSSOM

1¼ oz. Bacardi light rum
1 oz. orange juice
½ oz. lemon juice
½ tsp. sugar

BACARDI CHAMPAGNE COCKTAIL

1 oz. Bacardi silver rum
1 tsp. sugar
dash bitters
champagne to fill

Mix first three ingredients in a tall glass. Fill with champagne.

BACARDI COCKTAIL

3 parts Bacardi Superior rum
1 part lemon juice
1 tsp. grenadine
1 tbsp. sugar

Mix until ice has a consistency of sherbet. Serve in a stemmed cocktail glass.

BACARDI COLLINS

2 oz. Bacardi light rum
2 tsp. frozen lemonade or limeade (or juice of ½ lime or lemon)
½ tsp. sugar (1 tsp. if fresh lime or lemon juice is used)
club soda to fill
sliced fruit for garnish
cherry for garnish

Pour juices into a shaker over ice. Add sugar and Bacardi light rum. Shake well and pour into a tall glass. Fill with club soda and stir. Garnish with fruit slices and cherry.

BACARDI DAIQUIRI

1¼ oz. Bacardi light rum
½ oz. lemon juice
½ tsp. sugar

Mix in a shaker or blend with ice. Strain into a chilled cocktail glass or serve on the rocks. The original daiquiri was made with Bacardi rum in 1896.

BACARDI DRIVER

2 oz. Bacardi light rum
orange juice to fill
lime or lemon wedge

Pour Bacardi light rum into a tall glass over ice. Fill with orange juice. Squeeze and drop in a lime or lemon wedge. Stir.

BACARDI DRY MARTINI

2–3 oz. Bacardi dark or Gold Reserve rum
1 part dry vermouth
cherry for garnish

Stir with cracked ice and strain into a cocktail glass or pour over rocks. Garnish with cherry.

BACARDI EGGNOG BOWL

12 oz. Bacardi dark or Bacardi Gold Reserve rum
1 qt. fresh or canned eggnog
1 cup whipped heavy cream
grated nutmeg for garnish

Pour eggnog into a punch bowl. Add Bacardi dark or Bacardi Gold Reserve rum. Stir. Fold in whipping cream. Chill in refrigerator. Stir. Top individual servings with nutmeg and serve immediately. Serves 6.

BACARDI FIRESIDE

1¼ oz. Bacardi light or dark rum
1 tsp. sugar
hot tea to fill
1 cinnamon stick

Pour first two ingredients into a mug. Fill with very hot tea and add cinnamon stick. Stir.

BACARDI FIZZ

1¼ oz. Bacardi light rum
¼ oz. lemon juice
¼ oz. Rose's grenadine
soda to fill

Pour first two ingredients into a highball glass over ice. Add the grenadine and fill with soda.

BACARDI GIMLET

1 part Rose's lime juice
4 parts Bacardi light rum
thin slice lime for garnish

Stir over ice. Serve in cocktail glass with lime slice.

BACARDI HEMINGWAY

1½ oz. Bacardi light rum
juice of ½ lime
¼ oz. grapefruit juice
¼ oz. maraschino liqueur

Mix.

BACARDI HIGHBALL

2 oz. Bacardi light, dark, or Gold Reserve rum
club soda, water, or ginger ale to fill

Pour Bacardi over ice cubes in a highball glass. Fill with club soda, water, or ginger ale.

BACARDI KEY LARGO

1½ oz. Bacardi dark rum
2 oz. orange juice
1½ oz. Coco Lopez real cream of coconut
maraschino cherry for garnish

Garnish with a maraschino cherry.

BACARDI MAI TAI

½ oz. fresh lime juice
½ oz. orgeat syrup
½ oz. simple syrup
½ oz. orange curacao
1 oz. Bacardi light rum
½ oz. Bacardi 151 rum or 1 oz. Bacardi dark or Gold Reserve rum
mint sprig for garnish
pineapple stick for garnish
cherry for garnish

Pour first four ingredients into an old-fashioned or stem glass half-filled with finely cracked ice. Add Bacardi rums and stir gently once or twice. Garnish with mint sprig, pineapple stick, and a cherry. If desired, Mai Tai mix can be substituted for the first four ingredients.

BACARDI MANHATTAN

2–3 oz. Bacardi dark or Gold Reserve rum
1 oz. sweet vermouth
dash Angostura bitters
cherry for garnish

Stir with cracked ice and strain into a cocktail glass or pour over rocks. Garnish with cherry.

BACARDI MARGARITA

1 oz. Bacardi light rum
½ oz. triple sec
1 oz. fresh-squeezed lemon or lime juice
cracked ice
salt to rim glass

Moisten cocktail glass rim with lemon or lime rind. Dip rim in salt. Shake and strain into salt-rimmed glass.

BACARDI MARY

1½ oz. Bacardi light or dark rum
5 oz. tomato juice
squeeze of lemon or lime
dash Worcestershire sauce
pinch salt and pepper

Serve in a large glass over ice cubes. If desired, a prepared mix can be substituted for the last four ingredients.

BACARDI MONKEY WRENCH

2 oz. Bacardi light rum
grapefruit juice to fill

Pour Bacardi light rum into a tall glass over ice. Fill with grapefruit juice. Stir.

BACARDI NAVY GROG

⅔ oz. Bacardi light rum
1⅓ oz. Bacardi dark rum
1 oz. fresh lime or lemon juice
1 oz. orange juice
1 oz. pineapple juice
1 oz. passion fruit nectar
½ oz. Falernum syrup
mint sprigs for garnish

Blend with ½ cup finely cracked ice. Pour (unstrained) into a large old-fashioned glass half filled with finely cracked ice. Garnish with mint sprigs and serve with straws.

BACARDI OLD-FASHIONED

1 tsp. sugar
2 tsp. Angostura bitters
splash club soda
Bacardi dark or Gold Reserve rum
sliced fruit for garnish

Dissolve first three ingredients in an old-fashioned glass. Add 2 ice cubes and fill with Bacardi dark or Gold Reserve rum. Garnish with desired fruit slices.

BACARDI ORANGE DAIQUIRI

1½ oz. Bacardi light rum
½ oz. lime or lemon juice
1 oz. orange juice
1 tsp. sugar

Blend with ½ cup crushed ice. Serve in a chilled cocktail glass.

BACARDI PEACH DAIQUIRI

3 oz. Bacardi light rum
2 fresh peach halves, peeled (or 2 canned peach halves)
1 tsp. sugar (omit sugar if using canned peaches)
1 oz. lime or lemon juice

Blend with ½ cup crushed ice. Serve in chilled cocktail glasses. Serves 2. This is the official drink of the National Peach Council.

BACARDI PERFECT MANHATTAN

2–3 oz. Bacardi dark or Gold Reserve rum
½ part dry vermouth
½ part sweet vermouth
dash Angostura bitters
lemon or orange twist for garnish

Stir with cracked ice and strain into a cocktail glass or pour over rocks. Garnish with lemon or orange twist.

BACARDI PIÑA COLADA

1½ oz. Bacardi light or dark rum
1 oz. Coco Lopez real cream of coconut
2 oz. unsweetened pineapple juice

Blend with ½ cup ice or shake and serve over ice.

BACARDI PINEAPPLE DAIQUIRI

2 oz. Bacardi light rum
½ slice canned pineapple
1 tbsp. lime juice
1 tsp. sugar

Blend with ⅓ cup crushed ice. Serve in a chilled cocktail glass.

BACARDI PINK SQUEEZE

1½ oz. Bacardi light rum
pink lemonade to fill

Pour rum into a tall glass over ice and fill with pink lemonade.

BACARDI PLANTER'S PUNCH

3 oz. Bacardi dark or Gold Reserve rum
2 tsp. sugar
2 oz. lemon or lime juice
cherry for garnish
lemon or lime slice for garnish
½ orange, sliced, for garnish
mint sprig for garnish

Dissolve sugar in lemon or lime juice in a shaker. Fill with cracked ice and shake well. Strain into a 10-oz. glass over cracked ice. Garnish with cherry, lemon or lime slice, sliced orange, and a mint sprig. Serve with a straw.

BACARDI QUICK EGGNOG

5 oz. Bacardi dark or light rum
1 pint vanilla or eggnog ice cream
grated nutmeg for garnish

Blend. Sprinkle with nutmeg and serve immediately. Serves 6.

BACARDI RICKEY

2 oz. Bacardi light rum
½ lime or lemon
club soda to fill

Squeeze ½ lime or lemon and drop into a tall glass with ice. Add Bacardi light rum. Fill with club soda. Stir.

BACARDI SCORPION

7 oz. Bacardi light rum
⅓ oz. gin
⅓ oz. brandy
2 oz. orgeat syrup
2 oz. orange juice
4 oz. lemon juice
1 sprig mint

Pour into a pitcher and stir well. Add ice cubes and refrigerate at least an hour before serving in large champagne-type glasses. For a real Polynesian touch, float a gardenia on top. Serves 2.

BACARDI SINGLE EGGNOG

1 oz. Bacardi dark or light rum
1 egg
1 tsp. sugar
8 oz. milk
grated nutmeg for garnish

Shake vigorously with ice and strain into a tall glass. Sprinkle with nutmeg.

BACARDI SOMBRERO COOLER

2 oz. Bacardi light rum
3 oz. pineapple-grapefruit juice
orange, lemon, or lime slice for garnish

Pour over ice. Garnish with orange, lemon, or lime slice.

BACARDI STINGER

2 oz. Bacardi dark rum
1 oz. white crème de menthe

Shake with ice. Serve in a brandy snifter.

BACARDI STRAWBERRY COLADA

1½ oz. Bacardi light or dark rum
1 oz. Coco Lopez real cream of coconut
6 strawberries

Blend with ½ cup ice or shake and serve on ice.

BACARDI STRAWBERRY DAIQUIRI

1½ oz. Bacardi light rum
5 large fresh or frozen whole strawberries
1 tbsp. lime juice
1 tsp. sugar

Blend with ½ cup crushed ice. Serve in a chilled cocktail glass.

BACARDI SUNSET

1¼ oz. Bacardi light rum
orange juice
lime squeeze
orange wheel for garnish

Pour Bacardi light rum into a tall glass over crushed ice. Fill with orange juice and top with a lime squeeze. Garnish with orange wheel.

BACARDI SUPERIOR & GINGER ALE

1 part Bacardi Superior rum
4 parts ginger ale
lime wedge for garnish

Pour over ice in tall glass. Garnish with lime wedge.

BACARDI ZOMBIE

1 oz. Bacardi dark rum
2 oz. Bacardi light rum
1 oz. Bacardi 151 rum (plus ¼ oz. to float, optional)
1 oz. orange juice
1 oz. pineapple juice
juice of 1 lemon or lime
pineapple slice for garnish
cherry for garnish
1 tsp. powdered sugar (optional)

Shake with ice and pour into tall glass. Garnish with pineapple slice and cherry. If desired, float ¼ oz. Bacardi 151 and 1 tsp. powdered sugar on top.

BAHAMA MAMA

1½ oz. Whaler's Great White rum
1½ oz. Whaler's Vanille rum
1½ oz. Whaler's Rare Reserve rum
2 oz. pineapple juice
2 oz. orange juice
2 oz. sour mix
dash grenadine (optional)
maraschino cherries for garnish
orange slice for garnish

Shake well with ice. If using grenadine, add to the bottom of the serving glass before pouring. Pour into a chilled hurricane glass. Garnish with maraschino cherries, orange slice, and an umbrella.

BALI HAI

1 oz. Seven Tiki rum
½ oz. ginger liqueur
2 oz. lychee juice
2 oz. pineapple juice
4 mint leaves
mint sprig for garnish

Shake and pour into a highball glass. Garnish with a mint sprig.

BANAN-ALOHA KOOLER

2 oz. Whaler's Big Island banana rum
2 oz. orange juice
2 oz. pineapple juice
strawberry for garnish

Blend or shake with crushed ice. Pour into a cold glass. Garnish with strawberry.

BANANA APPEAL

2 oz. Whaler's Big Island banana rum
2 oz. milk
1 squirt chocolate syrup
1 scoop vanilla ice cream

BANANA BAY BREEZE

2 oz. Malibu Tropical banana rum
1 oz. pineapple juice
1 oz. cranberry juice
orange slice for garnish

Garnish with an orange slice.
    Developed by Sapa's, NYC.

BANANA CABANA COSMO

2 oz. Malibu Tropical banana rum
3 oz. tonic water
½ oz. cranberry juice
cherry for garnish

*Shake with ice and serve in a tall glass. Garnish with cherry.
Developed by Bamboo 52, NYC.*

BANANA COLADA

2 oz. Cruzan banana rum
1½ oz. coconut milk
1½ oz. pineapple juice

Blend with ice until smooth.

BANANA DAIQUIRI

1¼ oz. Bacardi light rum
¼ oz. lemon juice or Rose's lime juice
½ tsp. sugar
1 banana

Blend.

BANANA FIESTA

1 oz. Whaler's Big Island banana rum
1 oz. Two Fingers tequila
½ oz. triple sec
3 oz. sweet and sour mix
splash lime juice

Shake with ice and serve in a hurricane glass.

BANANA MAMA

1½ oz. light rum
½ oz. dark rum
1 oz. banana liqueur
1 oz. Coco Lopez real cream of coconut
1 oz. fresh or frozen strawberries
2 oz. pineapple juice

Blend.

BANANA MAN

1 oz. Bacardi light rum
¼ oz. Hiram Walker banana liqueur
½ oz. lemon juice or Rose's lime juice

Blend.

BANANA MILKSHAKE

1 oz. Gosling's gold rum
1 oz. Gosling's Black Seal rum
2 ripe bananas
1 oz. honey
1 cup milk
2 scoops vanilla ice cream
whipped cream for garnish
chocolate syrup for drizzling

Blend with ice and pour into a glass. Garnish with whipped cream. Drizzle chocolate syrup on top.

BANANA PUNCH FRAPPE

1 ½ oz. Bacardi light rum
¾ oz. orange juice
½ oz. banana liqueur

Blend.

BANANA RUM CREAM

1½ oz. Puerto Rican dark rum
½ oz. crème de bananes
1 oz. light cream

Shake well.

BANANA WITH MILK RUM

2 oz. Rhum Barbancourt 3 Stars
1 ripe banana
8½ oz. milk
2 tbsp. powdered sugar
1 egg yolk

Cut the banana into pieces. Beat the egg yolk. Blend all ingredients until a homogenous and consistent mixture is obtained. Pour into a glass and serve.

BARBADOS COCKTAIL

2 oz. Mount Gay rum
½ oz. Cointreau
½ oz. sweet and sour mix

Shake.

BARBADOS PUNCH

⅔ oz. Tommy Bahama Golden Sun rum
1 oz. Tommy Bahama White Sand rum
⅓ oz. premium orange liqueur
1¾ pineapple juice
1¾ orange juice
juice of ½ lime
2 dashes grenadine
orange slice for garnish
maraschino cherry for garnish

Pour all ingredients except Tommy Bahama Golden Sun rum into a shaker over ice. Shake sharply. Strain into a glass over ice. Carefully float Tommy Bahama Golden Sun rum on top. Garnish with slice of orange and maraschino cherry. Serve with a straw.

BARN RAISER

1 oz. light rum
1 oz. Boru vodka
½ oz. grenadine
2 oz. orange juice
2 oz. pineapple juice
¾ oz. Sea Wynde rum

Pour first five ingredients into a glass over ice. Float the Sea Wynde rum.

BAT BITE

1¼ oz. Bacardi Silver rum
¾ cup cranberry juice
1 lime or lemon wedge

Pour first two ingredients into a 10-oz. glass over ice. Squeeze and drop in lime or lemon wedge. Stir and serve.

BEACH BLONDE

2 oz. Wray & Nephew rum
½ oz. Warninks Advocaat
½ oz. fresh-squeezed orange juice
1 peeled banana
banana slice for garnish

Blend all ingredients with a scoop of crushed ice and pour into a Collins glass. Garnish with a banana slice.

BEACH BUM'S COOLER

¾ oz. light rum
1¼ oz. Irish cream
¼ oz. banana liqueur
1½ oz. Coco Lopez real cream of coconut
¼ oz. banana
2 scoops vanilla ice cream
maraschino cherry for garnish

Garnish with maraschino cherry.

BEACH PARTY

1¼ oz. Bacardi light or dark rum
1 oz. pineapple juice
1 oz. orange juice
1 oz. Rose's grenadine

Blend.

BEACHCOMBER

1½ oz. Puerto Rican white rum
¾ oz. Rose's lime juice
¼ oz. triple sec
dash maraschino liqueur

Shake.

BEACHCOMBER'S GOLDDUST

1½ oz. light rum
1 oz. lime juice
½ oz. triple sec
1 oz. Coco Lopez real cream of coconut
½ tsp. sugar

Blend.

BEACHCOMBER'S SPECIAL

1½ oz. Bacardi light rum
½ oz. orange curacao
¾ oz. lemon or lime juice
¼ tsp. sugar (optional)

Blend with crushed ice.

BEE BITE COCKTAIL

1 oz. light rum
juice of 2 limes
2 oz. orange juice
2 tsp. grenadine

Blend with crushed ice.

BEE'S KISS

1 oz. Puerto Rican white rum
¼ oz. Myers's dark rum
¾ oz. cream
2 tbsp. honey

Shake.

BELLA DONNA

1 oz. Gosling's Black Seal rum
1 oz. Disaronno amaretto
2 tbsp. fresh sour mix (combine 1 tbsp. each: sugar, water, lemon
  juice, lime juice)

Rim martini glass with sugar mix. Shake with ice. Strain into glass and serve.
   From the Las Vegas Bellagio Hotel.

THE BERMUDA DREAMSICLE

2 oz. Gosling's Black Seal rum
2 oz. Navan vanilla liqueur
2 oz. orange juice
1 scoop sherbet or orange twist for garnish

Shake vigorously with ice and strain into a martini glass. Garnish with a small scoop of sherbet or an orange twist.

BERMUDA TRIANGLE

1½ oz. Admiral Nelson's premium vanilla rum
2 oz. cranberry juice
2 oz. orange juice
orange slice for garnish

Stir gently over ice and garnish with a fresh orange slice.

THE BERMUDIAN

2 oz. Gosling's Gold Bermuda rum
2 oz. pineapple juice
¼ oz. Grand Marnier
2 fresh mint leaves, torn
lime twist for garnish

Shake vigorously and strain into a martini glass. Garnish with twist of lime.

BERRIES 'N' CREAM

½ oz. Captain Morgan Original spiced rum
¾ oz. wild berry schnapps
3 oz. strawberry cocktail mix
2 tbsp. raspberries or strawberries in syrup
2 oz. heavy cream
16 oz. scoop of crushed ice

BERRY MERRY CHRISTMAS

1 oz. RedRum
½ oz. blackberry brandy
5 oz. hot water
½ oz. lemon juice
¼ oz. grenadine
1 cinnamon stick

Combine first five ingredients in a mug and stir with the cinnamon stick.

BETWEEN THE SHEETS

½ oz. Pyrat XO Reserve rum
¼ oz. Citronge
½ oz. Cognac VSOP-Style
1 oz. fresh sweet and sour mix
lemon twist for garnish
sugar to rim glass

Shake and serve straight up in a glass with a sugar-coated rim. Garnish with a lemon twist.

BIG BAMBOO LOVE SONG

2 oz. Whaler's Rare Reserve rum
1 oz. Whalers's Great White rum
½ oz. triple sec
1 oz. pineapple juice
1 oz. orange juice
1 oz. lime juice
¾ oz. fruit syrup

Shake well with ice and pour into a Collins glass.

THE BIGWOOD GIRLS

¾ oz. Puerto Rican light rum
½ oz. brandy
½ oz. Cointreau or triple sec
½ oz. lemon juice

Shake.

BIKINI DAIQUIRI

¾ oz. Cruzan pineapple rum
¾ oz. Cruzan banana rum
2 oz. Coco Lopez real cream of coconut
1 oz. lime juice

Blend with crushed ice.

BLACK BEAUTY

1½ oz. Gosling's Black Seal rum
2–3 ripe blackberries
juice of ½ lime
1 sugar cube
2 dashes Peychaud bitters
2–3 oz. soda water

Muddle the blackberries, sugar cube, bitters, and lime juice. Add Gosling's Black Seal rum and shake with ice. Strain into a glass over fresh ice and top with soda water.
Created by the Old Sealbach Bar.

BLACK DEVIL

1½ oz. Puerto Rican light rum
½ oz. dry vermouth
1 pitted black olive

Stir well.

BLACK ELEPHANT

1 oz. Gosling's Black Seal rum
1 oz. Amarula cream liqueur

Pour over ice and stir.

BLACK JACK

Equal parts:
    Gosling's Black Seal rum
    Jack Daniels, chilled

BLACK MARIA

1 oz. Myers's dark rum
¾ oz. Tia Maria
1 tsp. sugar
1 cup cold coffee
lemon peel

Stir.

BLACK SEAL RUM RUNNER

1¼ oz. Gosling's Black Seal rum
¾ oz. blackberry liqueur
1 oz. banana liqueur
¾ oz. grenadine
½ oz. lime juice

Blend with crushed ice.

BLIGHTER BOB

1 oz. Puerto Rican light rum
½ oz. Puerto Rican dark rum
½ oz. créme de cassis
1 oz. orange juice
2 dashes orange bitters
2 oz. ginger ale
lemon twist

Stir.

BLING BLING

1 oz. RedRum
1 oz. Hypnotiq
2 oz. pineapple juice
2 oz. 7UP

Shake with ice and strain into a shot glass.

BLUE HAWAIIAN

1 oz. Tommy Bahama White Sand rum
1 oz. blue curacao
2 oz. pineapple juice
1 oz. coconut cream
pineapple slice for garnish
maraschino cherry for garnish

*Blend with a scoop of crushed ice until smooth. Strain into a glass.
Garnish with a slice of fresh pineapple and a maraschino cherry.*

BLUE HEAVEN

1 oz. light rum
1 oz. Hiram Walker blue curacao
1 oz. pineapple juice
1 tsp. Coco Lopez real cream of coconut

Blend with crushed ice.

BLUE LAGOON

1½ oz. Appleton Estate V/X Jamaica rum
4 oz. cranberry juice
lemon wedge for garnish

Stir with crushed ice. Serve in a cocktail glass and garnish with a wedge of lemon.

BLUE LIZARD

2 oz. Cruzan citrus rum
¾ oz. blue curacao
¼ oz. sweet and sour mix
¼ oz. Sprite or 7UP

Pour the first two ingredients into a glass over ice. Add sweet and sour and Sprite or 7UP. Stir and serve.

BLUE MARLIN

1 shot blue curaçao
1 shot Whaler's Great White rum
4 oz. lemon-lime mix
lime slice for garnish

Shake well over ice and strain into a chilled rocks glass. Garnish with lime slice.

BLUE PASSION

¾ oz. Captain Morgan Original spiced rum
½ oz. blue curacao
4 oz. sweet and sour mix
pineapple slice for garnish

Shake well with an 8-oz. scoop of crushed ice and serve in a Collins glass. Garnish with a pineapple slice.

BLUE SKY

¾ oz. Bacardi light rum
1½ oz. Canadian Mist
¾ oz. blue curacao
8 oz. pineapple juice
orange slice for garnish
maraschino cherry for garnish

Blend with crushed ice. Garnish with an orange slice and a maraschino cherry.

BLUE SUNSET

2 oz. Whaler's Pineapple Paradise rum
2 oz. pineapple juice
½ oz. blue curacao

Shake well and serve in a martini glass.

BLUE WATCH

¾ oz. Captain Morgan Original spiced rum
½ oz. blue curacao
4 oz. ginger ale

Pour over rocks in old-fashioned glass. Stir lightly.

BOB'S YOUR UNCLE

2 oz. Wray & Nephew rum
½ oz. Frangelico
½ oz. Cuarenta Tres liquor
¼ oz. Funkin liquid chocolate
¼ oz. white Mozart chocolate liquor
white chocolate for garnish

Lace chilled cocktail glass with white Mozart chocolate liquor. Shake all other ingredients and pour into the cocktail glass with Mozart chocolate liquor. Garnish with white chocolate.

THE BODEGA

2 oz. 10 Cane rum
2 oz. Coco Lopez real cream of coconut
2 oz. mango nectar
2 oz. guava nectar

Combine all ingredients in a mixing glass. Add ice and shake vigorously. Strain into a chilled classic daiquiri glass. May also be served unstrained in a rocks glass.
Created by: Robert Ryan, New York City mixologist.

BOGART'S AFRICAN QUEEN

3 oz. Starr African rum
3 oz. Alizé passion fruit

Shake well over ice and strain into a martini glass.

BOLERO

1½ oz. Rhum Barbancourt
½ oz. Calvados
2 tsp. sweet vermouth
dash bitters

Stir. Serve straight up or on the rocks.

BONBINI

1 oz. Bacardi light or dark rum
¼ oz. Hiram Walker orange curaçao
2 dashes Angostura bitters

Stir.

BONE SHAKER

2 oz. VooDoo spiced rum
½ oz. triple sec
½ oz. lime juice
3 oz. pineapple juice
lime wedge for garnish

Blend with crushed ice. Garnish with lime wedge.

BONGO DRUM

1 oz. Bacardi light rum
¼ oz. Hiram Walker blackberry-flavored brandy
pineapple juice to fill

Pour rum into a tall glass half filled with ice. Fill with pineapple juice. Float brandy on top.

BONSAI COLADA

3 oz. Whaler's Pineapple Paradise rum
1 oz. Burnett's orange vodka
1 oz. coconut cream
pineapple slice for garnish

Shake with ice and strain or pour into a hurricane glass. Garnish with pineapple slice.

BORINQUEN

1½ oz. light rum
1 tbsp. passion fruit syrup
1 oz. lime juice
1 oz. orange juice
1 tsp. 151-proof rum

Blend at low speed with ½ cup crushed ice. Pour into an old-fashioned glass.

BOSSA NOVA

2 oz. dark rum
1½ oz. Liquore Galliano
1 oz. apricot brandy
3 oz. passion fruit juice

BOSTON BREEZE

1¼ oz. rum
1 oz. Coco Lopez real cream of coconut
3 oz. cranberry juice cocktail

Blend with crushed ice.

BOSTON COOLER

2 oz. light rum
juice of ½ lemon
1 tsp. powdered sugar
2 oz. club soda
club soda or ginger ale to fill
orange spiral or lemon peel for garnish

Pour first three ingredients into a Collins glass and stir. Fill with cracked ice and add rum. Fill with club soda or ginger ale and stir again. Garnish with a spiral of orange or lemon peel and dangle end over rim of glass.

BOSTON SIDECAR

¾ oz. light rum
¾ oz. brandy
¾ oz. triple sec
juice of ½ lime

Shake with ice and strain into a cocktail glass.

BRAND NEW TATTOO

2 oz. Sailor Jerry Navy spiced rum
7UP to fill
splash orange juice

Pour Sailor Jerry Navy spiced rum into a glass and fill with 7UP. Mix. Add a splash of orange juice.

BRIDGETOWN

2 oz. Cockspur Fine rum
splash cherry juice
dash sweet vermouth
cherry for garnish

Shake with ice. Serve in a cocktail glass. Garnish with cherry.

BRINLEY COFFEE ON THE ROCKS

3 oz. Brinley gold coffee rum
crushed ice
fresh coffee bean for garnish

Garnish with coffee bean.

BRINLEY CREAMSICLE

2 oz. Brinley vanilla rum
2 oz. orange juice
1 oz. milk

Shake well and pour into a glass over ice.

BRINLEY LIME FIZZ

3 parts Brinley Gold lime rum
4 parts club soda or lemon-lime soda
lime wedge for garnish

Pour into a tall glass over ice. Garnish with lime wedge.

BRINLEY "SPIKED" HOT COCOA

3 oz. Brinley Gold vanilla rum
4 oz. hot hot chocolate
1 marshmallow (or 6 small marshmallows)
chocolate shavings for garnish

Serve piping hot in a big mug. Top off with marshmallow and dark chocolate shavings.

BROWN DERBY

1¼ oz. Puerto Rican dark rum
½ oz. lime juice
⅙ oz. maple syrup

Shake.

BUBBLES & MANGO

1 oz. mango puree
2 oz. Flor de Cana 7-year-old rum
¾ oz. fresh-squeezed lime juice
½ oz. simple syrup
1½ oz. Prosecco

Shake first four ingredients and strain into a 6-oz. martini glass. Top with Prosecco.

BUCK-A-ROO

1¼ oz. Bacardi light or dark rum
root beer to fill

Pour rum into a highball glass over ice. Fill with root beer.

BUCK JONES

1½ oz. light rum
1 oz. sweet sherry
juice of ½ lime
ginger ale to fill

Pour first three ingredients into a highball glass over ice cubes and stir. Fill with ginger ale.

BULLDOG COCKTAIL

1½ oz. Bacardi light or dark rum
¾ oz. lime juice
½ oz. cherry-flavored brandy
maraschino cherry for garnish

Garnish with maraschino cherry.

BURGUNDY BISHOP

1 oz. light rum
juice of ¼ lemon
1 tsp. powdered sugar
red wine to fill
fresh fruit for garnish

Shake with ice and strain into a highball glass over ice cubes. Fill with red wine and stir. Decorate with fruits.

BUSHRANGER

1 oz. Puerto Rican white rum
1 oz. Dubonnet
2 dashes Angostura bitters

Stir.

BUSHWHACKER

½ oz. rum
2 oz. Coco Lopez real cream of coconut
1 oz. coffee-flavored liqueur
½ oz. dark crème de cacao
2 oz. half and half

Blend with 1 cup ice until smooth.

BWI SWIZZLE

2 oz. Pyrat XO Reserve rum
½ oz. Marie Brizard Apry liqueur
1 oz. Rock Candy syrup or simple syrup
juice of 1 lime
2 dashes Angtostura bitters

Pour into a 14-oz. goblet ¾ full with crushed ice. Put a swizzle between the palms of your hands and swizzle, adding crushed ice until the drink is frothing and the outside of the glass frosts.

THE CAESAR'S KISS

½ oz. Bacardi vanilla rum
1 oz. Tequila Rose
½ oz. Baileys Irish cream
½ oz. Chambord
strawberry whipped cream for garnish

Shake. Serve in a rocks glass. Garnish with strawberry whipped cream.

CAFE RUMBA

1 oz. Kahlua
1 oz. Whaler's Vanille rum
hot coffee to fill
whipped cream to top

Pour first two ingredients into a mug. Fill with coffee. Top with whipped cream and enjoy.

CAIPIRISSIMA

2 oz. Pyrat Superior Blanco rum
1 small lime, cut into quarters
1 heaping tsp. brown sugar

In a 16-oz. mixing glass muddle the lime and brown sugar together until juice has been extracted and the sugar dissolved. Fill with cracked (not crushed) ice, then add Pyrat Superior Blanco rum. Shake until well blended and pour into a double old-fashioned glass. Add more ice if needed.

CALIFORNIA FIZZ

1½ oz. Bacardi light or dark rum
4 oz. orange juice
club soda to top

Pour first two ingredients into a tall glass. Top with club soda.

CALM BEFORE THE STORM

2½ oz. Tommy Bahama Golden Sun rum
juice of ½ lime
ginger beer to top
lime wheel for garnish

Pour first two ingredients into a bucket glass over ice. Top with ginger beer. Garnish with lime wheel.

CALM VOYAGE

1 oz. Bacardi light rum
¼ oz. Hiram Walker apple-flavored brandy
1 oz. orange juice
dash bitters

Shake with ice and serve on the rocks.

CALYPSO COOL-AID

1¼ oz. Rhum Barbancourt
1 oz. pineapple juice
½ oz. lemon or lime juice
¼ tsp. sugar
club soda to top

Blend first four ingredients. Top with club soda. Garnish with pineapple spear and lime wheel.

CALYPSO COOLER

½ oz. Captain Morgan Original spiced rum
¼ oz. Myers's Original dark rum
½ oz. peach schnapps
2 oz. orange juice
1 oz. grenadine
1 oz. lime juice
2 oz. lemon-lime soda
orange slice for garnish

Shake first six ingredients well and pour into a Collins or specialty glass over ice. Top with lemon-lime soda. Garnish with an orange slice.

CANA BRAVA

2 oz. Flor de Cana Gold 4-year-old rum
3 oz. Bloody Mary mix
½ oz. jalapeno juice
½ oz. lime juice

Stir over ice.

CANA DORADA MARTINI

½ oz. sweetened lime juice
1½ oz. Flor de Cana gold 7-year-old rum
½ oz. triple sec
1 oz. orange juice

Shake and serve in a martini glass.

CANA-SUTRA

2 oz. Flor de Cana extra-dry 4-year-old rum
1 oz. cranberry juice
1 oz. pineapple juice
1 oz. peach schnapps
1 oz. grenadine

Shake and serve on the rocks.

THE CANARY

1½ oz. 10 Cane rum
1½ oz. anisette
2½ oz. fresh-squeezed pineapple juice
crème de cacao to rim glass
brown sugar to rim glass
1 star anise for garnish

Rim a martini glass with crème de cacao and brown sugar. Pour 10 Cane, anisette, and pineapple juice into a shaker with ice. Shake vigorously and strain into the martini glass. Garnish with a floating star anise. Recline in an armchair.
Created by the Elbow Beach Resort bartender team, Bermuda.

CANITAS

2 oz. 10 Cane rum
1 shot espresso
sugar to taste (optional)
1 tsp. fresh whipped cream (optional)

In a small shot or juice glass add 10 Cane and espresso. Add sugar, if using. Garnish with fresh whipped cream, if desired.

CANNONBALL

1–2 oz. Gosling's Black Seal rum
½ oz. Rose's lime cordial
Equal parts (to top):
   cranberry juice
   pineapple juice
   orange juice
orange wheel for garnish
cherry for garnish

Pour the first two ingredients into a glass. Top with equal parts cranberry, pineapple, and orange juice. Garnish with orange wheel and cherry.

CAPTAIN MORGAN DAIQUIRI

1 oz. Captain Morgan Original spiced rum
¼ oz. cherry liqueur
1 oz. sweet and sour mix
lime wheel for garnish

Shake vigorously over crushed ice and strain into a stemmed cocktail glass. Garnish with lime wheel.

CAPTAIN MORGAN SOUR

1 ¼ oz. Captain Morgan Original spiced rum
1 oz. fresh-squeezed lemon juice
1 tsp. sugar

Shake and serve on the rocks.

CAPTAIN'S COLADA

1¼ oz. Captain Morgan Original spiced rum
5 oz. piña colada mix
pineapple stick for garnish
maraschino cherry for garnish

Blend with crushed ice until smooth. Pour into specialty glass. Garnish with pineapple stick and a maraschino cherry.

CAPTAIN'S CRUISER

1 ¼ oz. Captain Morgan Parrot Bay rum
3 oz. orange juice
2 oz. pineapple juice

Mix in a shaker. Pour into a tall glass over ice.

CAPTAIN'S PEARL

1 oz. Captain Morgan Original spiced rum
¼ oz. amaretto
1½ oz. half and half
½ ripe banana

Blend with a scoop of crushed ice.

CAPTAIN'S TROPICAL SPICED TEA

1¼ oz. Captain Morgan Original spiced rum
3 oz. iced tea
½ tsp. lemon juice
2 oz. ginger ale
lemon wheel for garnish

Stir in a highball glass over ice. Garnish with a lemon wheel.

CARIBBEAN COCOA

1½ oz. Coruba Jamaica rum
hot cocoa to fill
whipped cream for garnish
chocolate curls for garnish

Pour Coruba rum into a mug. Fill with hot cocoa. Garnish with whipped cream and top with chocolate curls.

CARIBBEAN COOLER

1 oz. Captain Morgan Original spiced rum
¼ oz. white créme de cacao
3 oz. orange juice
1½ oz. club soda

Pour rum, créme de cacao, and orange juice over ice in a glass. Stir. Add soda and stir gently.

CARIBBEAN CRUSH

3 oz. coconut milk
⅓ ripe banana
½ oz. Baileys Irish cream
1½ oz. Pyrat XO Reserve rum
1 scoop of ice
whipped cream for garnish
shredded coconut for garnish

Blend for 15–20 seconds. Garnish with whipped cream and shredded coconut.

CARIBBEAN DATE

1½ oz. Pyrat XO Reserve rum
1 oz. tangerine puree
1 oz. Thai coconut milk
cinnamon and demerara sugar to rim glass
mint sprig for garnish

Shake with ice and strain into a chilled cocktail glass rimmed with cinnamon-demerara sugar. Garnish with a fresh mint sprig.

CARIBBEAN JOY

1½ oz. Bacardi light rum
1 oz. pineapple juice
¾ oz. lemon juice

Shake and serve on the rocks.

CARIBBEAN PASSION

½ oz. Mount Gay rum
¾ oz. Passoã
1 oz. pineapple juice
splash orange juice

Shake. Serve in a tall glass over ice.

CARIBBEAN QUEEN

1¼ oz. Bacardi Limón rum
½ oz. Cointreau
2 oz. orange juice
3 oz. Coco Lopez real cream of coconut

Blend with ice. Serve in a martini glass.

CARIBBEAN ROMANCE

3 oz. Bacardi light rum
1½ oz. sugar syrup
2 pieces papaya
2 pieces banana
1 oz. lime juice
1 oz. Coco Lopez real cream of coconut
orange slice for garnish
pineapple slice for garnish
cherry for garnish

Blend. Garnish with orange slice, pineapple slice, and cherry.

CARIBBEAN SEA

1½ oz. Appleton Estate V/X Jamaica rum
¾ oz. blue curacao
3 oz. pineapple juice
1½ oz. coconut cream

Mix in a Collins glass over ice.

CARIBBEAN SHOOTER

¾ oz. Captain Morgan Original spiced rum
½ oz. brandy
1 oz. cranberry juice

Shake with ice and strain into a glass.

CARIBBEAN SUNSET

¾ oz. Whaler's Great white rum
¾ oz. Burnett's gin
¾ oz. blue curaçao
¾ oz. banana liqueur
1 oz. lemon juice
1 oz. lime juice
dash grenadine
lime slice for garnish

Shake first six ingredients over ice and pour into a cocktail glass. Add grenadine and garnish with lime slice.

CARIBE COCKTAIL

1¼ oz. Captain Morgan Original spiced rum
1 oz. pineapple juice
½ oz. lemon juice
lime wedge for garnish

Shake with ice cubes and strain into a stemmed cocktail glass. Garnish with lime wedge.

CARNIVAL COOLER

2 oz. Fernandes "19" white rum
¾ oz. lime juice
2 dashes Angostura bitters
club soda to fill

Pour first three ingredients into a Collins glass over ice and stir. Fill with club soda.

CASABLANCA

2 oz. Captain Morgan Original spiced rum
½ oz. créme de noya
¼ oz. apricot liqueur
4 oz. orange juice
½ oz. simple syrup

Serve in a glass with a 6-oz. scoop of crushed ice.

CHAMBORD COLADA

1½ oz. Bacardi rum
1½ oz. Chambord
2 oz. pineapple juice
½ oz. Coco Lopez real cream of coconut

Blend with ice. Serve in a tall glass.

CHAMPAGNE TIKI

1 oz. Pyrat XO Reserve rum
1 oz. Cruzan banana rum
1 oz. fresh strawberry coulis
juice of ½ lime
champagne to top
grated nutmeg for garnish
mint sprig for garnish

Shake first four ingredients and strain into a 7 ½-oz. stem glass. Top with champagne. Garnish with a sprinkle of nutmeg and fresh mint sprig.

CHAYOTE SPECIAL

1½ oz. Bacardi light rum
3 drops blue curacao
1½ oz. sour apple
green apple slice for garnish

Shake with cracked ice until cold. Serve in a chilled martini glass and garnish with a slice of green apple.
   From the Chayote Restaurant.

CHERRIED CREAM RUM

1½ oz. Rhum Barbancourt
½ oz. cherry brandy
½ oz. light cream

Shake.

CHERRY PASSION POTION

1 oz. white rum
1½ oz. cherry juice
1½ oz. passion fruit juice
stem-on maraschino cherry dipped in dark chocolate for garnish

Blend. Serve in a rocks glass over ice. Garnish with chocolate-dipped maraschino cherry. This drink is a 1999 Maraschino Cherry Contest Winner.
  Dolores Long, Van Nuys, CA.

CHERRY POP

1 oz. Malibu rum
½ oz. peach schnapps
½ oz. orange juice
5 cherries
½ oz. maraschino cherry juice
whipped cream for garnish
maraschino cherry for garnish

Blend with one scoop of ice. Garnish with a dollop of whipped cream and a maraschino cherry. This drink is a 1999 Maraschino Cherry Contest Winner.
  Mark Langell, Staten Island, NY.

CHICAGO STYLE

¾ oz. Bacardi light rum
¼ oz. Hiram Walker triple sec
¼ oz. Hiram Walker anisette
¼ oz. lemon or Rose's lime juice

Shake. Serve over ice.

CHINESE COCKTAIL

1½ oz. Jamaica rum
1 tbsp. grenadine
1 dash bitters
1 tsp. maraschino
1 tsp. triple sec

Shake with ice and strain into a cocktail glass.

CHOCOLADA

2 oz. Bacardi light rum
1½ oz. Coco Lopez real cream of coconut
1½ oz. milk
1 oz. dark crème de cacao
whipped cream for garnish
chocolate chips for garnish

Blend with 1 cup ice. Garnish with whipped cream and chocolate chips.

CHOCOLATE CAKE

¾ oz. Whaler's coconut rum
¾ oz. white créme de cacao
¼ oz. hazelnut liqueur
splash half-and-half
whipped cream for garnish

Shake and strain into an old-fashioned glass over ice. Garnish with whipped cream.

CHOCOLATE COLADA

2 oz. rum
2 oz. Coco Lopez real cream of coconut
2 oz. half-and-half
1 oz. chocolate syrup

Blend with 1 cup crushed ice. Serve in a tall glass.

CHOCOLATE-COVERED STRAWBERRY

1 oz. rum
½ oz. Kahlúa
½ oz. triple sec
10 strawberries

Blend with crushed ice. Serve in a cocktail glass.

CHRISTMAS CHEER

1½ oz. Newfoundland Screech rum
3 oz. eggnog
grated nutmeg for garnish

Pour into a glass over ice, stir, and top with a sprinkle of nutmeg. Light the fire, hang the stockings, and wait for good ol' St. Nick.

CHUNKY MONKEY MARTINI

2 oz. Cruzan rum cream
1 oz. Cruzan banana rum
¼ oz. dark crème de cacao

Pour first two ingredients into a mixing glass with ice and add dark crème de cacao. Stir and strain into a martini glass.

CINNAMON TOAST

1¼ oz. Captain Morgan Original spiced rum
6 oz. hot apple cider
sugar and cinnamon to rim glass

Rim glass with sugar and cinnamon. Add hot cider and rum. Blend with crushed ice until slushy.

CITRUS SQUEEZE

2 oz. 267 mango rum
1 oz. 267 orange vodka

Serve on the rocks with an orange wedge on the side.

CLAM VOYAGE

1 oz. Bacardi light or dark rum
¼ oz. apple-flavored brandy
1 oz. orange juice
dash orange bitters

THE CLASSIC HURRICANE

2 oz. Sailor Jerry Spiced Navy rum
1 tbsp. passion fruit syrup
2 tsp. lime juice

Shake with ice and strain into a cocktail glass.

COC AMOR

1½ oz. CocoRibe rum
½ oz. amaretto
2 oz. lemon juice
maraschino cherry for garnish

Shake with ice; serve in a tall glass with maraschino cherry.

COCKSPUR BAJAN SUNSET

1 oz. Cockspur fine rum
2 oz. cranberry juice
2 oz. orange juice
lime slice for garnish

Serve over ice and garnish with a slice of lime.

COCKTAIL TROPIQUE

3 parts White Rhum de Martinique
½ part syrup of cane
1 part syrup of grenadine
2 parts lemon juice

Shake with ice.

COCO COW

1 oz. Captain Morgan Original spiced rum
1 oz. cream of coconut
2 oz. half and half

Blend with 1 cup crushed ice until smooth and pour into a glass.

COCO LOPEZ LIMÓN MADNESS

½ oz. Bacardi Limón rum
½ oz. Coco Lopez real cream of coconut
1 oz. orange juice
1 oz. cranberry juice

Blend with crushed ice. Serve in a tall glass.

COCO LOPEZ LIMÓNADE

1 oz. Bacardi Limón rum
3 oz. Coco Lopez lemonade

Blend with crushed ice.

COCO LOPEZ PURPLE PASSION

1½ oz. Bacardi light rum
3 oz. Coco Lopez purple passion colada mix

Blend with crushed ice.

COCO NAUT

2 oz. Wray & Nephew rum
2 oz. Coco Lopez real cream of coconut
¼ oz. fresh-squeezed lime juice

Blend with crushed ice and serve in a tumbler.

COCO POM

¼ oz. Captain Morgan Parrot Bay coconut rum
1½ oz. Smirnoff No. 21 vodka
2 oz. pomegranate juice
1 tsp. coconut flakes

Shake first three ingredients over ice and strain into a chilled martini glass. Top with coconut flakes.

COCOA BANANA TINI

1¼ part Malibu Tropical banana rum
¾ part Hiram Walker white cacao
¾ part half-and-half
banana slice for garnish
cinnamon for garnish

Shake and strain into a martini glass. Garnish with a banana slice and cinnamon sprinkles.

COCOA BEACH

1½ Prichards's Crystal rum
4 oz. orange juice
2 oz. pineapple juice
1 oz. piña colada mix

Blend with 3/4 cup ice until slushy.

COCOBANA

1 part Bacardi light rum
1 banana
1 part coconut milk

Blend with crushed ice.
    Susan McGowan, Oddfellows Restaurant.

COCOMOTION

1½ oz. Puerto Rican dark rum
4 oz. Coco Lopez real cream of coconut
2 oz. lime juice

Blend with 1 ½ cups ice.

COCONUT BANANA COLADA

2 oz. Cruzan coconut rum
¾ oz. Cruzan banana rum
2 oz. Coco Lopez real cream of coconut
3 oz. pineapple juice

Blend with crushed ice.

COCONUT BROWNIE

1¼ oz. Captain Morgan Original spiced rum
¼ oz. hot chocolate
1 tsp. whipped cream

Pour first two ingredients into a mug and top with whipped cream.

COCONUT CLOUD MARTINI

1 oz. Tommy Bahama White Sand rum
½ oz. vanilla vodka
½ oz. coconut rum
½ oz. Coco Lopez real cream of coconut
toasted coconut for garnish

Shake with ice. Garnish with toasted coconut.

COCONUT COLADA

1¼ oz. Captain Morgan Parrot Bay coconut rum
1 oz. milk
5 oz. pineapple juice
pineapple spear for garnish

Blend 10–15 seconds and pour into a specialty glass. Garnish with a pineapple spear.

COCONUT GROVE

1 oz. rum
2 oz. Coco Lopez real cream of coconut
1 oz. orange juice

Blend with crushed ice.

COCONUT HONEY

1 oz. dark rum
2 oz. Coco Lopez real cream of coconut
1 oz. honey

Blend with crushed ice.

COFFEE CREAM COOLER

1¼ oz. Bacardi light or dark rum
cold coffee to fill
cream to taste

Pour Bacardi light or dark rum into a tall glass half filled with ice. Fill with cold coffee and cream to taste.

THE COLONIALIST

2 oz. 10 Cane rum
1½ oz. dark crème de cacao
fresh cream to top

Combine all ingredients. Add ice and shake vigorously. Strain into a chilled martini glass. Top with a layer of fresh cream.

COLUMBUS COCKTAIL

1½ oz. Puerto Rican golden rum
juice of ½ lime
¾ oz. apricot brandy

Serve over crushed ice.

COMPOSITION

2 oz. La Mauny white rum
½ oz. Marie Brizard Ananas
½ oz. Marie Brizard mango liqueur
3 oz. orange juice

Shake and strain into a tall glass over ice.

CONTINENTAL

1 oz. Bacardi light rum
¼ oz. Hiram Walker green créme de menthe
¾ oz. Rose's lime juice
¼ tsp. sugar (optional)

Stir. Serve over ice.

CORKSCREW

¾ oz. Bacardi light rum
¼ oz. Asbach Uralt brandy
¼ oz. port wine
½ oz. lemon or Rose's lime juice

Stir. Serve over ice.

CORUBA CANE

2 oz. Coruba Jamaica rum
½ oz. lemon-lime soda
½ oz. grenadine
2 oz. strawberry daiquiri mix
1 oz. orange juice
orange wedge for garnish
cherry for garnish

Blend with ice until slushy. Pour into a tall glass and garnish with an orange wedge and a cherry.

COQUITO

1 ½ oz. Pyrat XO Reserve rum
1 oz. coconut milk
1 oz. orange juice
1 egg yolk

Shake and serve in a small white wine glass, straight up. Garnish with ground cinnamon and an orange twist.

COW PUNCHER

1 oz. Bacardi light or dark rum
1 oz. Hiram Walker white créme de cacao
milk to fill

Pour rum and créme de cacao into a tall glass half filled with ice. Fill with milk.

CRAN-RUM TWISTER

2 oz. Puerto Rican light rum
3 oz. cranberry juice
lemon-lime soda to fill
lime slice for garnish

Pour into a tall glass over ice. Garnish with lime slice.

CRANBERRY KISS

¾ oz. Captain Morgan Original spiced rum
2 oz. Collins mix
2 oz. cranberry juice
lemon wedge for garnish

Stir in a highball glass over ice. Garnish with lemon wedge.

CRANBERRY MINT RICKEY

2½ oz. 10 Cane rum
2 tbsp. cranberries (fresh or frozen)
1 oz. fresh-squeezed lime juice
splash club soda
3 mint leaves
cranberries for garnish
mint sprig for garnish

In a mixing glass, muddle cranberries and macerate with simple syrup and 10 Cane for 10 minutes. Add mint leaves and muddle gently. Add lime juice,and ice, and stir. Strain into rocks glass with ice. Top with club soda. Garnish with cranberries and mint sprig.

CREAM PUFF

1½ oz. Bacardi light rum
2 oz. cream
½ oz. crème de Noyeaux (or almond-flavored liqueur)

Shake with ice. Serve in a martini glass.

CREAM SODA

1¼ oz. Captain Morgan Original spiced rum
¼ oz. triple sec
1 oz. lime juice
2 oz. pineapple juice
lemon slice for garnish

Pour into a tall glass over ice. Stir well. Garnish with lemon slice.

CREAMY SMOOTH EGGNOG PUNCH

1 bottle (750 ml) Don Q gold rum
12 egg yolks
½ lb. confectioner's sugar
1 qt. milk
1 qt. heavy cream
grated nutmeg for garnish

Beat egg yolks until light (or use your favorite eggnog mix). Beat in sugar until mixture thickens. Stir in milk and Don Q gold rum. Chill 3 hours. Pour into a punch bowl and fold in cream, stiffly whipped. Chill 1 hour and dust with nutmeg. Serves 24.

CREOLE

1¾ oz. Puerto Rican white rum
3–4 ice cubes
2 splashes lemon juice
3½ oz. beef bouillon
pepper to taste
salt to taste
Tabasco to taste
Worcestershire sauce to taste

Shake. Serve on the rocks.

CRICKET

¾ oz. Bacardi light rum
¼ oz. Hiram Walker white créme de cacao
¼ oz. Hiram Walker green créme de menthe
1 oz. cream

Shake. Serve over ice.

CROW'S NEST

1½ oz. Admiral Nelson's Premium vanilla rum
1½ oz. Arrow melon liqueur
3 oz. piña colada mix
3 oz. sour mix

Blend with ice.

CRUZAN CHEESECAKE MARTINI

2 oz. Cruzan vanilla rum
1 oz. pineapple juice
1 oz. cranberry juice

Shake with ice and strain into a martini glass.

CRUZAN GIMLET

2 oz. Cruzan white rum
1 tbsp. sweetened lime juice
lemon or lime slice for garnish

Shake briskly with ice and strain into a cocktail glass. Garnish with lemon or lime slice.

CRUZAN ISLAND MIST

2 oz. Cruzan white or gold rum
lemon peel twist

Pour into a small old-fashioned glass packed with crushed ice. Serve with short straws.

CRUZAN MAI TAI

1½ oz. Cruzan white rum
½ oz. Cruzan gold rum
½ oz. lime juice
½ oz. blue curaçao
½ oz. orgeat syrup
1 tsp. superfine sugar
pineapple stick for garnish
cherry for garnish

Pour into an old-fashioned glass over cracked ice. Stir well. Garnish with pineapple stick and a cherry. Serve with straws.

THE CRUZAN SUZAN

½ oz. Cruzan rum
⅓ oz. white crème de cacao
juice of 1 orange

Shake. Pour into a goblet over shaved ice.

CRYSTAL PUNCH

1½ oz. Prichards' Crystal rum
4 oz. orange juice
2 oz. pineapple juice
1 oz. piña colada mix

Blend with ¾ cup ice until smooth.

CUBA LIBRE

1 ¾ oz. Bacardi rum
cola to taste
¼ lime

Pour Bacardi rum into a glass and fill with cola to taste. Add lime. Stir.

DARK 'N' DARING

1 shot Alnwick rum
cola to fill

Pour Alnwick rum into a tall glass over ice and fill with cola.

DARK 'N' STORMY

1½ oz. Gosling's Black Seal rum
3 oz. ginger beer
lemon wedge to rim glass
lemon wedge for garnish

Serve in a tall glass over ice. Squeeze a lemon wedge around the rim of the glass. Garnish with lemon wedge.
    Bermuda's National Drink.

DARK SECRETS

1 shot Alnwick rum
1 bottle of Fentimans ginger beer
lime squeeze

Pour into a tall glass over ice in order listed above. Squeeze in fresh lime.

DEAD ELVIS

2 oz. RedRum
½ oz. 151 rum (to float)
½ oz. apricot brandy
1 oz. pineapple juice
½ oz. lime juice
2 oz. orange juice
1 tsp. superfine sugar
cherry for garnish
orange slice for garnish

Blend all ingredients except 151 rum with 1 cup ice. Strain into a cocktail glass. Float the 151 rum. Garnish with cherry and orange slice. Serve with a straw.

DEPAZ APRICOT COLLINS

1½ oz. Depaz Blue Cane amber rum
4 tsp. apricot preserves
½ oz. fresh lemon juice
¾ oz. Crème Peche
1 oz. fresh orange juice
half-wheel orange slice for garnish

Shake vigorously with ice. Strain into a highball glass over fresh ice. Garnish with orange slice.

DERBY DAIQUIRI

2 oz. Whaler's Great White rum
½ oz. Hypnotiq
1 oz. lime juice
½ teaspoon simple syrup (recipe follows)
lime wedge for garnish
mint sprig for garnish

Shake vigorously with ice and strain into a cocktail glass. Garnish with lime wedge and mint sprig.

To make simple syrup: Bring 1 cup water to a boil. Add 2 cups sugar. When the sugar is fully dissolved, remove from heat and allow to cool. Store in a plastic squeeze bottle.

DEVIL'S TAIL

1 ½ oz. light rum
1 oz. vodka
2 tsp. apricot brandy
2 tsp. grenadine
½ oz. lime juice

Shake with ice and serve over ice.

DON Q CELEBRATION PUNCH

1 bottle (750 ml) Don Q gold rum
16 oz. orange juice
16 oz. unsweetened pineapple juice
1 32-oz. bottle club soda
3 oz. lime juice
confectioner's sugar to taste

Pour first five ingredients into a punch bowl over ice. Stir gently. Add sugar to taste. Serves 12 to 15.

DON Q CHAMPAGNE PUNCH

1 bottle (750 ml) Don Q gold rum
3 pineapples
1 1-lb. pkg. confectioner's sugar
2 cups lemon juice
½ cup Arrow curaçao liqueur
½ cup maraschino cherry juice
4 bottles (750 ml each) chilled champagne

Peel, core, and slice the pineapples. Crush or chop slices into a large container. Dissolve sugar and lemon juice and add to pineapple. Add curaçao, cherry juice, and Don Q gold rum. Chill 2 hours. Pour into a punch bowl over ice, add champagne, and stir gently. Serves 20.

DON Q HOLIDAY PUNCH

1 bottle (750 ml) Don Q light rum
½ cup lemon juice
¼ cup confectioner's sugar
1 cup orange juice
1 cup cranberry juice
1 cup strong tea
12 cloves
8 lemon slices
10 maraschino cherries

In a punch bowl, mix lemon juice and sugar. Add orange juice, cranberry juice, and tea. Pour in Don Q light rum. Add cloves, lemon slices, cherries, and ice cubes to chill. Serves 15.

DRUNKEN MONKEY

1½ oz. Gosling's Black Seal rum
½ oz. banana liqueur
4 oz. pineapple juice
pineapple wedge for garnish

Shake vigorously on ice and strain into a martini glass. Garnish with pineapple wedge.

DUB DEVIL

2 oz. Wray & Nephew rum
2 tsp. orgeat syrup
2 dashes Angostura bitters
3 oz. apple juice
3 lime squeezes

Build the first two ingredients over cubed ice. Top with apple juice. Add Angostura bitters and lime squeezes.

DYN-O-MITE DAIQUIRI

2 oz. rum
3 oz. orange banana liqueur
½ oz. triple sec
1 oz. lime juice

Shake with ice and serve over ice.

EASTER COCKTAIL

1 oz. white Barbancourt rum
½ oz. triple sec
1 oz. Advocaat
1 oz. orange juice
soda water to top

Pour first four ingredients into a glass over ice. Top with soda water and stir well.

THE ECLIPSE

1½ oz. Mount Gay rum
1 oz. pineapple juice
1 oz. orange juice

Shake.

EL CONQUISTADOR

1¼ oz. Don Q Crystal rum
5 oz. pineapple juice
¼ oz. triple sec
½ oz. raspberry liqueur
orange slice for garnish
cherry for garnish

Garnish with a slice of orange and a cherry.
    From the El Conquistador Hotel.

ELUSIVE REDHEAD

1½ oz. Appleton Estate V/X Jamaica rum
3 oz. Clamato or Bloody Mary mix
horseradish to taste
Tabasco to taste
black pepper to taste
sea salt to taste
Worcestershire sauce to taste
lime juice to taste
celery stick for garnish
olives for garnish

Pour into a highball glass rimmed with sea salt and/or pepper. Season to taste with horseradish, Tabasco, pepper, salt, Worcestershire sauce, or lime juice. Garnish with a celery stick and olives.

EXTRA AND GINGER

1½ oz. Appleton Estate V/X Jamaica rum
6 oz. ginger ale
orange or lemon wedge for garnish

Serve in a tall glass over ice. Garnish with orange or lemon wedge.

FALLING LEAVES

1 oz. Gosling's Black Seal rum
½ oz. Marie Brizard raspberry liqueur
dash grenadine
4 oz. orange juice

Serve in a tall glass.

FANNY'S FAVORITE

½ oz. Admiral Nelson's raspberry rum
½ oz. Admiral Nelson's coconut rum
½ oz. Arrow melon liqueur
½ oz. Arrow raspberry liqueur
splash pineapple juice
splash white soda
orange twist for garnish
cherry for garnish

Mix first five ingredients and pour into a glass over ice. Top with white soda and garnish with a twist of orange and a cherry.

FIREMAN'S SOUR

1½ oz. Bacardi light rum
1½ oz. lemon or lime juice
½ tsp. sugar
¼ oz. grenadine
club soda to top
maraschino cherry for garnish
lemon or lime wheel for garnish

Blend first four ingredients and top with club soda. Garnish with a maraschino cherry and a lemon or lime wheel.

FLAMINGO

1½ oz. Rhum Barbancourt
juice of ¼ lime
several dashes grenadine
1 oz. pineapple juice

Shake with ice and serve on the rocks.

FLIRTING WITH THE SANDPIPER

1½ oz. Puerto Rican light rum
½ oz. cherry brandy
3 oz. orange juice
2 dashes orange bitter

Stir well.

FLOR FUSION

1 oz. Flor de Cana 4-year-old extra-dry rum
1 oz. Flor de Cana 7-year-old gold rum
½ oz. fresh lime juice
½ oz. orange juice
½ oz. pineapple juice
½ oz. cranberry juice
¼ oz. simple syrup
dash bitters
2 sweet Amarena cherries for garnish

Shake with ice and strain over fresh ice into a highball glass. Garnish with cherries.

FROZEN BERKELEY

2 oz. light rum
½ oz. brandy
1 tbsp. passion fruit syrup
1 tbsp. lime juice

Shake and serve over ice.

FROZEN TROPICAL SPLIT

1¼ parts Malibu Tropical banana rum
¾ part Hiram Walker white cacao
1 part strawberry puree
2 parts piña colada mix
strawberry for garnish
banana slice for garnish

Blend with ice until smooth. Garnish with strawberry and banana slice.

FROZEN TROPICAL STRAWBERRY MARGARITA

1 part Malibu Tropical banana rum
¾ part Tezon Blanco tequila
½ parts strawberry puree
½ parts fresh sour mix
strawberry for garnish
banana slice for garnish

Blend with ice until smooth. Garnish with strawberry and banana slice.

FLORIDITA

1½ oz. Bacardi light rum
1 oz. orange juice
½ oz. triple sec

Shake and serve over ice.

FLUKE

1 oz. Whaler's spiced rum
½ oz. Hypnotiq cordial
5 oz. cola
cherry for garnish

Pour into a cocktail glass over ice. Garnish with cherry.

FLYING KANGAROO

1 oz. Rhum Barbancourt
1 oz. vodka
¼ oz. Liquore Galliano
½ oz. cream
¾ oz. coconut cream
1½ oz. pineapple juice
¾ oz. orange juice

Shake.

FORBIDDEN PLEASURE

1½ oz. Mount Gay Eclipse rum
½ fresh banana
1½ oz. Ponche Kuba
2½ oz. cream of coconut
2 oz. pineapple juice
mint sprig for garnish

Blend with ice and garnish with mint sprig.

FOUR SEASONS STARR MARTINI

2 oz. Starr African rum
2 oz. ginger ale
splash passion fruit puree
tiny dash Cointreau
fresh raspberry for garnish

Shake well with ice and strain into a martini glass. Garnish with a fresh raspberry.

FOURSQUARE PIÑA COLADA

1 oz. Foursquare spiced rum
5 oz. pineapple juice (plus more to taste)
1½ oz. coconut cream
cherry for garnish

Blend well at high speed with 1 cup crushed ice. Pour into a Collins glass and garnish with a cherry and pineapple juice to taste.

FRENCH COLADA

1½ oz. Puerto Rican white rum
¾ oz. sweet cream
¾ oz. Coco Lopez real cream of coconut
1½ oz. pineapple juice
splash cassis
¾ oz. cognac

Blend with 1 scoop crushed ice.

FRENCH CONNECTION

1 oz. Newfoundland Screech rum
1 oz. Dubonnet
lemon slice for garnish

Pour over ice and stir. Garnish with slice of lemon. Parlez-vous frança

FROSTY FRIAR

¾ oz. white rum
1½ oz. Frangelico liqueur
1 scoop strawberry ice cream

Blend with ice.

FROZEN WHITE-CAP

1½ oz. Appleton Estate V/X rum
2 oz. pineapple juice
1 tbsp. lime juice

Blend with 1 scoop crushed ice.

FUNKY PYRAT

1½ oz. Pyrat XO Reserve rum
4 oz. apricot brandy
dash Herbsaint
2 oz. fresh sweet and sour
splash grenadine
orange twist for garnish
mint sprig for garnish

Shake and strain over ice. Garnish with orange twist and fresh mint sprig.

FUZZY CHARLIE

¾ oz. Captain Morgan Original spiced rum
¾ oz. peach schnapps
2 oz. piña colada mix
4 oz. orange juice
1 slice pineapple
mint sprig for garnish

Pour into a glass over ice and stir. Garnish with mint sprig.

FUZZY MANGO

2 oz. Brinley mango rum
3 oz. lemon-lime soda
orange peel for garnish

Serve in a tall glass and garnish with orange peel.

GANGRENE

1½ oz. RedRum
3 oz. pineapple juice
½ oz. melon liqueur
cherry for garnish

Mix first two ingredients over ice in a tall glass. Float melon liqueur. Garnish with cherry.

GERMAN CHOCOLATE MARTINI

½ oz. Captain Morgan Parrot Bay coconut rum
½ oz. Godiva original liqueur
½ oz. Smirnoff black cherry vodka
¼ oz. German chocolate shavings

Shake first three ingredients with ice and strain into martini glass. Garnish with German chocolate shavings.

FLORIDITA

1½ oz. Bacardi light rum
1 oz. orange juice
½ oz. triple sec

Shake and serve over ice.

FLUKE

1 oz. Whaler's spiced rum
½ oz. Hypnotiq cordial
5 oz. cola
cherry for garnish

Pour into a cocktail glass over ice. Garnish with cherry.

FLYING KANGAROO

1 oz. Rhum Barbancourt
1 oz. vodka
¼ oz. Liquore Galliano
½ oz. cream
¾ oz. coconut cream
1½ oz. pineapple juice
¾ oz. orange juice

Shake.

FORBIDDEN PLEASURE

1½ oz. Mount Gay Eclipse rum
½ fresh banana
1½ oz. Ponche Kuba
2½ oz. cream of coconut
2 oz. pineapple juice
mint sprig for garnish

Blend with ice and garnish with mint sprig.

FOUR SEASONS STARR MARTINI

2 oz. Starr African rum
2 oz. ginger ale
splash passion fruit puree
tiny dash Cointreau
fresh raspberry for garnish

Shake well with ice and strain into a martini glass. Garnish with a fresh raspberry.

FOURSQUARE PIÑA COLADA

1 oz. Foursquare spiced rum
5 oz. pineapple juice (plus more to taste)
1½ oz. coconut cream
cherry for garnish

Blend well at high speed with 1 cup crushed ice. Pour into a Collins glass and garnish with a cherry and pineapple juice to taste.

FRENCH COLADA

1½ oz. Puerto Rican white rum
¾ oz. sweet cream
¾ oz. Coco Lopez real cream of coconut
1½ oz. pineapple juice
splash cassis
¾ oz. cognac

Blend with 1 scoop crushed ice.

FRENCH CONNECTION

1 oz. Newfoundland Screech rum
1 oz. Dubonnet
lemon slice for garnish

Pour over ice and stir. Garnish with slice of lemon. Parlez-vous français?

FROSTY FRIAR

¾ oz. white rum
1½ oz. Frangelico liqueur
1 scoop strawberry ice cream

Blend with ice.

FROZEN BERKELEY

2 oz. light rum
½ oz. brandy
1 tbsp. passion fruit syrup
1 tbsp. lime juice

Shake and serve over ice.

FROZEN TROPICAL SPLIT

1¼ parts Malibu Tropical banana rum
¾ part Hiram Walker white cacao
1 part strawberry puree
2 parts piña colada mix
strawberry for garnish
banana slice for garnish

Blend with ice until smooth. Garnish with strawberry and banana slice.

FROZEN TROPICAL STRAWBERRY MARGARITA

1 part Malibu Tropical banana rum
¾ part Tezon Blanco tequila
1½ parts strawberry puree
1½ parts fresh sour mix
strawberry for garnish
banana slice for garnish

Blend with ice until smooth. Garnish with strawberry and banana slice.

FROZEN WHITE-CAP

1½ oz. Appleton Estate V/X rum
2 oz. pineapple juice
1 tbsp. lime juice

Blend with 1 scoop crushed ice.

FUNKY PYRAT

1½ oz. Pyrat XO Reserve rum
4 oz. apricot brandy
dash Herbsaint
2 oz. fresh sweet and sour
splash grenadine
orange twist for garnish
mint sprig for garnish

Shake and strain over ice. Garnish with orange twist and fresh mint sprig.

FUZZY CHARLIE

¾ oz. Captain Morgan Original spiced rum
¾ oz. peach schnapps
2 oz. piña colada mix
4 oz. orange juice
1 slice pineapple
mint sprig for garnish

Pour into a glass over ice and stir. Garnish with mint sprig.

FUZZY MANGO

2 oz. Brinley mango rum
3 oz. lemon-lime soda
orange peel for garnish

Serve in a tall glass and garnish with orange peel.

GANGRENE

1½ oz. RedRum
3 oz. pineapple juice
½ oz. melon liqueur
cherry for garnish

Mix first two ingredients over ice in a tall glass. Float melon liqueur. Garnish with cherry.

GERMAN CHOCOLATE MARTINI

½ oz. Captain Morgan Parrot Bay coconut rum
½ oz. Godiva original liqueur
½ oz. Smirnoff black cherry vodka
¼ oz. German chocolate shavings

Shake first three ingredients with ice and strain into martini glass. Garnish with German chocolate shavings.

GINGER COLADA

½ oz. rum
1½ oz. Coco Lopez real cream of coconut
1 oz. Canton Delicate ginger liqueur

Blend with 1 cup ice.

GINGER SMASH

1½ oz. 10 Cane rum
¾ oz. Luxardo maraschino cherry liqueur
¾ oz. Berentzen apple liqueur
½ oz. fresh-squeezed lime juice
2 matchbox-size pieces of fresh pineapple
2 long, thin slices of fresh ginger root
1 tsp. bar sugar
pineapple leaf for garnish

Muddle pineapple, ginger, and sugar into a consistent paste in the bottom of a mixing glass. Add the rest of the ingredients and fill the mixing glass halfway with ice. Shake briefly and pour unstrained into a rocks or old-fashioned glass. Garnish with a pineapple leaf.
Best selling 2007 summer cocktail at Employees Only, NYC.

GINGER SNAP

¾ oz. Captain Morgan Original spiced rum
½ oz. ginger brandy
4 oz. eggnog
ginger snap for garnish (optional)

Blend to desired consistency and pour into a glass. Garnish with a ginger snap for dunking if desired.

GOLD CURE

2 oz. Wray & Nephew rum
1 oz. honey
½ oz. hot water
juice of 1 lime
lime twist for garnish

Mix honey in hot water until fully dissolved. Add Wray & Nephew rum and lime juice. Add cubed ice and shake. Strain into a chilled cocktail glass. Garnish with a twist of lime.

GOLDEN GOOSE

5 oz. Brut champagne
1 oz. unsweetened pineapple juice
½ oz. Gosling's Gold Bermuda rum
pineapple stick for garnish

Mix first two ingredients in a champagne flute. Gently float Gosling's Gold Bermuda rum on top, allowing it to slowly mingle. Garnish with a slim stick of pineapple.

GOLDEN SUNSET

1½ oz. Tommy Bahama Golden Sun rum
1 oz. premium orange liqueur
burnt orange twist for garnish

Pour into a snifter over ice and mix well. Garnish with burnt orange twist.

GOSLING'S ORANGE CIDER MARTINI

3 oz. Gosling's Gold Bermuda rum
1 tsp. cinnamon-sugar mix
orange wedge
3 oz. mulled cider, chilled
¼ oz. orange juice
¼ oz. Cointreau
orange twist for garnish

Place cinnamon-sugar in a dish. Rub orange wedge around the rim of a martini glass and dip rim into cinnamon-sugar. Shake remaining ingredients over ice and strain into rimmed martini glass. Garnish with an orange twist.
Created by Ming Tsai, Blue Ginger Restaurant.

GRAPE PUNCH

1¼ oz. Bacardi light rum
grape juice to fill
lime or lemon wedge

Pour Bacardi light rum into a tall glass over ice. Fill with grape juice and add a squeeze of lime or lemon.

GRASSHOPPER

1 oz. Bacardi light rum
¼ oz. Hiram Walker green créme de menthe
½ oz. cream

Blend with crushed ice.

GRAVE DIGGER

½ oz. Stroh 80 rum
½ oz. Malibu rum
½ oz. Midori
3 oz. pineapple juice

Serve over ice in a tall glass.
    From Rum Jungle at Mandalay Bay.

GREAT WHITE

1 oz. Whaler's Great White rum
1 oz. cranberry juice
4 oz. orange juice
lemon wedge for garnish

Pour ingredients into a cocktail glass over ice. Garnish with a lemon wedge.

GREEN MONKEY

1½ oz. Malibu Tropical banana rum
¾ part melon liquor
1½ oz. fresh sour
1½ oz. pineapple juice

Shake with ice. Serve over ice.

GREEN PARROT

1½ oz. Appleton Estate V/X rum
4 oz. orange juice
1 oz. blue curacao
orange slice for garnish

Pour ingredients, one at a time in the order listed above, into a large stemmed glass over ice. Do not mix. Garnish with an orange slice.

GUAYAVITA

1½ oz. Flor de Caña Grand Reserve 7-year-old rum
1 oz. guava pulp
2 oz. sour mix

Shake and serve on the rocks.

HAPPY ENDINGS' GILLIGAN

1 oz. Malibu coconut rum
1 oz. Malibu mango rum
1 oz. Malibu tropical banana rum
½ oz. cranberry juice
½ oz. pineapple juice
cherry for garnish

Shake with ice and serve on the rocks. Garnish with cherry.
   Developed by Happy Endings, New York.

HARD HAT

1¼ oz. Bacardi Silver rum
1¼ oz. fresh lime juice
1 tsp. sugar
¼ oz. Rose's grenadine
club soda to fill

Shake first three ingredients with ice and strain into a 10-oz. glass. Fill with club soda.

HAVANA BANANA FIZZ

2 oz. light rum
2½ oz. pineapple juice
1½ oz. fresh lime juice
3–5 dashes Peychaud's bitters
⅓ banana, sliced
bitter lemon soda to fill

Blend first five ingredients. Fill with bitter lemon soda.

HAVANA SIDECAR

1½ oz. Puerto Rican golden rum
¾ oz. lemon juice
¾ oz. triple sec

Mix with 3–4 ice cubes.

HAVANA SPECIAL

2 oz. white rum
1 tbsp. maraschino cherry liqueur
½ tbsp. sugar
1 oz. lemon or lime juice

Shake and serve on the rocks.

HAWAIIAN DAISY

1½ oz. Bacardi light rum
1 oz. pineapple juice
¼ oz. lemon or lime juice
¼ oz. grenadine
club soda to top

Pour first four ingredients into a glass and top with club soda.

HAWAIIAN HULA

1½ parts Malibu Tropical banana rum
¾ part guava nectar
¾ part fresh sour mix
orange corkscrew for garnish

Shake and strain into a martini glass. Garnish with orange corkscrew.

HAWAIIAN NIGHT

1 oz. Bacardi light rum
¼ oz. Hiram Walker cherry-flavored brandy
pineapple juice to fill

Pour Bacardi light rum into a tall glass half filled with ice. Fill with pineapple juice and float cherry-flavored brandy on top.

HAWAIIAN PLANTATION COBBLER

1½ oz. Pyrat XO Reserve rum
½ oz. Citronge liqueur
1½ oz. fresh sweet and sour
½ oz. simple syrup
½ slice of peeled pineapple
ginger ale
mint sprig for garnish
crystallized ginger for garnish

Shake first five ingredients. Fill with ginger ale, then pour into a glass over ice. Garnish with fresh mint sprig and crystallized ginger.

HEMINGWAY DAIQUIRI

1½ oz. 10 Cane rum
½ oz. Luxardo maraschino cherry liqueur
1 oz. fresh-squeezed grapefruit juice
½ oz. fresh-squeezed lime juice
½ oz. simple syrup
lime wheel for garnish
black cherry for garnish

Combine all ingredients in a mixing glass. Add ice and shake vigorously. Strain into a chilled cocktail glass. Garnish with a lime wheel and a black cherry on a skewer.

HOLY BANANA COW

1 oz. Shango rum
1 oz. crème de banana
1½ oz. cream
dash grenadine
banana slice for garnish
grated nutmeg for garnish

Shake with crushed ice and strain into a glass. Top with a slice of banana and sprinkle lightly with nutmeg.

HOT BUTTERED RUM

1 oz. Whaler's Vanille rum, per serving
1 cup sugar
1 cup brown sugar
1 cup butter
2 cups vanilla ice cream
¾ cup boiling water, per serving
grated nutmeg for garnish

Combine sugars and butter in a 2-quart saucepan. Cook over low heat, stirring until butter is melted. Combine cooked mixture with ice cream in large mixing bowl and beat at medium speed until smooth. Store refrigerated up to 2 weeks or frozen up to a month. For each serving, fill ¼ of a mug with mixture, and add 1 oz. Whaler's Vanille Rum and ¾ cup boiling water. Sprinkle with nutmeg.

HOT RUM AND CIDER PUNCH

1 bottle (750 ml) Don Q light rum
½ gallon apple cider
cloves for garnish
lemon slices for garnish
cinnamon sticks for garnish

Pour Don Q light rum into a bowl and add heated apple cider. Stir. Garnish with lemon slices stuck with cloves. Add a cinnamon stick to each punch cup to enhance flavor. Serves 12.

HOT VOODOO DADDY

1 oz. VooDoo spiced rum
½ oz. butterscotch schnapps
5 oz. hot chocolate
whipped cream to top

Combine first three ingredients in a mug and top with whipped cream.

HOURGLASS

1½ oz. Admiral Nelson's Premium spiced rum
4 oz. orange juice
splash grenadine

Serve over ice.

HUMMER

1 oz. Admiral Nelson's Premium spiced rum
1 oz. Caffe Lolita coffee
2 scoops vanilla ice cream

Blend with crushed ice and serve in a decorative glass.

HURRICANE ANDREW

1 oz. Cockspur Five Star colored rum
1 oz. Cockspur white rum
1 oz. orgeat syrup
1 oz. passion fruit juice
3 oz. orange juice
½ oz. lime juice
maraschino cherries for garnish
orange slice for garnish

Shake well with ice and pour into a chilled hurricane glass. Garnish with maraschino cherries, an orange slice, and an umbrella.

ICE BREAKER

½ oz. Myers's Original dark rum
¼ oz. créme de noya
¼ oz. cognac
¼ oz. gin
2 oz. lemon juice
1 oz. orange juice

Shake.

IN THE PINK

1¼ oz. Myers's Original rum cream
1 oz. Coco Lopez real cream of coconut
1 tsp. grenadine

Blend with ice.

INDIFFERENT MISS

¾ oz. Captain Morgan Original spiced rum
¾ oz. lime juice
1 tsp. simple syrup
3 oz. club soda

Pour the rum, juice, and syrup over ice in a glass. Stir. Add the soda and stir gently.

INTERNATIONAL MAI TAI

½ oz. Malibu rum
½ oz. Myers's Original dark rum
½ oz. rum
1 tsp. orgeat syrup
2 oz. pineapple juice
2 oz. sweet and sour mix

Blend with ice. Serve in a tall glass.

ISLA GRANDE ICED TEA

1½ oz. Puerto Rican dark rum
3 oz. pineapple juice
3 oz. unsweetened brewed iced tea
lemon or lime slice for garnish

Pour into a tall glass with ice. Garnish with a lemon or lime slice.

ISLAND SUNSET

1 oz. Whaler's Rare Reserve rum
1 oz. Whaler's Great White rum
1 tbsp. passion fruit syrup
2 tsp. lime juice
dash grenadine
lime wedge for garnish

Shake and pour into a chilled hurricane glass over ice. Garnish with lime wedge.

ISLAND VOODOO

1½ oz. VooDoo spiced rum
1½ oz. RedRum
2 oz. guava juice
2 oz. mango juice
½ oz. fresh lime juice
½ oz. fresh lemon juice

Blend with ice and serve in a tall glass.

ITALIAN COLADA

1½ oz. Puerto Rican white rum
¾ oz. sweet cream
¼ oz. Coco Lopez real cream of coconut
2 oz. pineapple juice
¼ oz. amaretto

Blend with 1 scoop crushed ice.

JADE

1½ oz. Puerto Rican white rum
¾ oz. lime juice
1 tbsp. sugar
dash triple sec
dash green créme de menthe

Shake. Serve over ice.

JAMAICA SNOW

1¼ oz. rum
½ oz. blue curaçao
2 oz. Coco Lopez real cream of coconut
2 oz. pineapple juice

Blend with 2 cups ice.

JAMAICAN HOLIDAY

1⅓ oz. Appleton Estate V/X Jamaica rum
½ peach (peeled or canned)
juice of ½ lime
1 tsp. sugar
peach wedge for garnish

Blend with 1 scoop crushed ice. Serve in a cocktail glass. Garnish with a peach wedge.

JAMAICAN SHAKE

1 shot Myers's Original dark rum
½ shot blended whiskey
2 oz. milk or cream

Blend with ice.

JAMAICAN SUNSET

2 oz. Wray & Nephew rum
2 oz. cranberry juice
3 oz. fresh-squeezed orange juice

Shake all ingredients with ice and strain into an ice-filled Collins glass.

JAMAICAN WAKE-UP CALL

1½ oz. Appleton Estate V/X Jamaica rum
hot black coffee to fill
whipped cream to top

Pour Appleton Estate V/X Jamaica rum into a coffee mug. Fill with coffee and top with whipped cream.

JEALOUS LOVER

2 oz. Starr African rum
3 large strawberries
½ oz. fresh lime juice
½ oz. pineapple juice
¾ oz. simple syrup

Muddle strawberries. Shake with ice and strain into a martini glass.

JONESTOWN COOL-AID

2 oz. RedRum
½ oz. pineapple juice
½ oz. cranberry juice

Shake with ice. Serve as a cocktail or shots.

JUMBLE BREW

1 oz. Cruzan coconut rum
1 oz. Cruzan pineapple rum
3 oz. orange juice
lime squeeze

Mix first three ingredients and add a squeeze of lime. Pour into a tall glass over ice. Garnish with an exotic flower.

JUMP UP AND KISS ME

½ oz. Sea Wynde rum
½ oz. Liquore Galliano
½ oz. Marie Brizard's Apry apricot liqueur
dash Dr. Swami & Bone Daddy's gourmet sweet and sour mix
orange juice
pineapple juice

Shake first five ingredients with ice and strain into a Collins glass. Fill with orange juice and pineapple juice.

JUMP UP BANANA-NANA

⅓ cup Cruzan banana rum
1 med. banana
1 lime, squeezed
1 tbsp. honey or fine powdered sugar
1 tsp. vanilla extract
pineapple wedge for garnish
cherry for garnish

Blend with 2 cups crushed ice until smooth. Pour into a stemmed glass and garnish with a pineapple wedge and a cherry.

JUNGLE FLAME

2 oz. Starr African rum
fresh lemon wedge
¼ oz. simple syrup
lemon-lime soda

Cut up lemon and place pieces in a mixer with ice, Starr African rum, and syrup. Pour into a highball glass. Top with lemon-lime soda.

THE KAHLUA COLADA

½ oz. rum
1 oz. Coco Lopez real cream of coconut
2 oz. pineapple juice
1 oz. Kahlúa

Blend with 1 cup ice.

KEY LIME DREAM

1½ oz. light rum
¾ oz. Rose's lime juice
2 scoops vanilla ice cream

Blend with ice.

KEY WEST SONG

1¼ oz. Captain Morgan Original spiced rum
1 oz. cream of coconut
2 oz. orange juice

Blend until smooth with 1 cup ice and pour into a glass.

KILLA' COLA

2 oz. Whaler's Killer coconut rum
½ oz. Hypnotiq
4 oz. cola
cherry for garnish

Pour into a cocktail glass over ice and garnish with a cherry.

KILLER COLADA

3 oz. Whaler's Killer coconut rum
3 tbsp. coconut milk
3 tbsp. crushed pineapples
pineapple wedge for garnish
2 cherries for garnish

Blend at high speed with 2 cups crushed ice. Pour into a chilled hurri-cane glass and garnish with pineapple wedge and cherries.

KILLER MAI TAI

1 oz. RedRum
1 oz. VooDoo spiced rum
2 oz. orange juice
2 oz. pineapple juice
¼ oz. grenadine
½ oz. dark rum
cherry for garnish

Pour RedRum and VooDoo spiced rum into a glass over ice. Top with juices and grenadine. Float dark rum and garnish with cherry.

"KILLER" RITA

2 oz. Whaler's Killer coconut rum
1 oz. triple sec
1 oz. pineapple juice
½ oz. coconut milk
salt to rim glass
maraschino cherries for garnish

Rim a margarita glass with salt. Mix and pour into margarita glass over ice. Garnish with maraschino cherries.

KINGSTON COFFEE

4 oz. fresh-brewed coffee
1 oz. Myers's rum
dollop whipped cream
powdered bittersweet chocolate for sprinkling
cinnamon stick for garnish

Pour first two ingredients into a coffee cup or mug. Top with whipped cream and sprinkle powdered bittersweet chocolate on top. Garnish with a cinnamon stick.

KINGSTON COSMO

2 oz. Appleton Estate V/X Jamaica rum
½ oz. Cointreau
splash cranberry juice
lime squeeze

Pour first two ingredients into a glass. Top with cranberry juice and lime squeeze.

KINGSTON SOUR

1½ oz. Wray & Nephew rum
fresh pear slice (plus another for garnish)
½ oz. apple juice
½ oz. apricot brandy
dash sour mix
⅛ oz. crème de cassis

Muddle first three ingredients, then shake hard with all other ingredients over ice. Strain into an ice-filled highball glass. Garnish with a pear slice.

KOKO-COLA

1½ oz. Cruzan coconut rum
2 oz. soda
squeeze lime

Mix with ice and serve on the rocks.

KON-TIKI

1½ oz. Seven Tiki rum
2 oz. mango nectar
2 oz. cranberry juice
dash absinthe

Pour into a highball glass with ice. Stir.

LABADU

3 oz. Malibu rum
3 oz. pineapple juice
1 oz. milk or vanilla ice cream

Blend with ice.

LADY HAMILTON

1½ oz. Pusser's rum
1 tsp. fresh lime juice
Equal parts:
   passion fruit juice
   orange juice
   ginger ale

LAUGHTER

1½ oz. Cockspur Old Gold rum
1 oz. lime juice
1 tsp. sugar
3–4 mint leaves
club soda to top

Combine lime juice, mint, and sugar in a Collins or highball glass. Stir gently to bruise the mint. Fill glass ¾ with ice. Add the Cockspur Old Gold rum. Top with soda. Stir well.

LIGHT 'N STORMY

2 oz. 10 Cane rum
3–4 oz. ginger beer
½ oz. fresh-squeezed lime juice
lime wedge for garnish
candied ginger for garnish

Fill a highball glass ¾ full with ice. Combine all ingredients and stir. Garnish with lime wedge and candied ginger.

LIME FIZZ

2 oz. Brinley gold lime rum
3 oz. club soda (or lemon-lime soda if you like it sweeter)
1 lime wedge

Pour first two ingredients into a glass. Squeeze in and garnish with lime wedge.

LIME LUAU

1 oz. Whaler's Big Island banana rum
2 oz. vodka
dash lime juice
dash orange syrup

Stir with ice and serve in cocktail glass.

LIMÓN MERINGUE PIE SHOT DRINK

2 oz. Bacardi Limón rum
1 oz. Disaronno Originale amaretto
powdered sugar
ready-to-use whipped cream (preferably in a can)

Have someone sprinkle powdered sugar on your tongue, then take a drink of Bacardi Limón topped with Disaronno amaretto, but don't swallow. Have someone spray whipped cream in your mouth, then shake and swallow a little slice of pie.

LOVE POTION

1 oz. rum
½ oz. banana liqueur
½ oz. triple sec
1 oz. orange juice
1 oz. pineapple juice
orange slice for garnish
pineapple slice for garnish
banana slice for garnish

Garnish with orange, pineapple, and banana slices.

LOVE STICK

2 oz. Cockspur Five Star colored rum
1 oz. Cockspur white rum
½ oz. triple sec
1 oz. pineapple juice
1 oz. orange juice
1 oz. lime juice
¾ oz. fruit syrup

Shake well with ice. Pour into a tall glass.

LUCKY LADY

¾ oz. Bacardi light rum
¼ oz. Hiram Walker anisette
¼ oz. Hiram Walker white créme de cacao
¾ oz. cream

MALIBU ACOMPÁÑAME

2 parts Malibu coconut rum
1 part Hiram Walker triple sec
splash fresh lime juice

MALIBU AFTER TAN

1 part Malibu coconut rum
1 part white crème de cacao
2 scoops vanilla ice cream

Blend with ice and serve in a specialty glass.

MALIBU BANANA COW

1½ parts cream
1 part Malibu Tropical banana rum
1 part Malibu coconut rum
dash grenadine
grated nutmeg for sprinkling
banana slices for garnish

Shake and strain into a cocktail glass. Sprinkle with nutmeg and garnish with banana slices.
   Developed by Orchid Lounge, NYC.

MALIBU BANANA-BERRY SPLIT

1 part Malibu Tropical banana rum
1 part Stoli Razberi vodka
lemon juice
simple syrup

Shake with ice and serve in a shot glass.
   Developed by Sapa's, NYC.

MALIBU BANANA MANGO BREEZE

1 part Malibu Tropical banana rum
1 part Malibu mango rum
1 part fresh sour mix
1 part cranberry juice

MALIBU BANANA PADDY

1 part Malibu Tropical banana rum
1 part Kahlúa
splash peppermint schnapps

Developed by 40C, NYC.

MALIBU BANANA SPLIT

1 part Malibu Tropical banana rum
splash amaretto
splash crème de cacao
whipped cream for garnish
cherry for garnish

Garnish with whipped cream and a cherry.
Developed by Orchid Lounge, NYC.

MALIBU BANANA TROPIC-TINI

1½ parts Malibu Tropical banana rum
½ part peach schnapps
dollop mango puree
splash passion fruit nectar
cherry for garnish

Shake and serve as a martini. Garnish with a cherry.
Developed by Happy Ending Bar, NYC.

MALIBU BANANA ZINGER

2 oz. Malibu Tropical banana rum
2 scoops lemon sherbet
2 oz. sour mix
lemon wedge for garnish

Mix in blender with 2 cups ice. Garnish with lemon wedge. Makes 2 drinks.
   Developed by Zombie Hut, NYC.

MALIBU BEACH

1½ oz. Malibu rum
1 oz. Smirnoff vodka
4 oz. orange juice

Serve over ice.

MALIBU BLUE LAGOON

1 part Malibu coconut rum
4 parts pineapple juice
¾ part blue curaçao

MALIBU CARIBENO

3 parts Malibu coconut rum
1 part Martel cognac
½ part pineapple
½ part fresh lemon juice
lemon wedge for garnish

Serve on the rocks. Garnish with a lemon wedge.

MALIBU COCO COLADA MARTINI

3 parts Malibu coconut rum
1 part Hiram Walker triple sec
½ part Coco Lopez real cream of coconut
½ part fresh lime juice
lime wedge for garnish

Serve in a martini glass. Garnish with lime wedge.

MALIBU COCO-COSMO

2 parts Malibu coconut rum
splash triple sec
splash pomegranate juice
splash cranberry juice
dash lime juice
lime twist for garnish

Shake with ice and strain into a martini glass. Garnish with lime twist.
Developed by Bamboo 52, New York.

MALIBU COCO-LIBRE

1 part Malibu coconut rum
3 parts cola
lime slice for garnish

Serve over ice in a tall glass. Garnish with a lime slice.

MALIBU COCONUT CREAMSICLE

2 parts Malibu coconut rum
1 scoop frozen vanilla yogurt
orange juice to fill

Pour first two ingredients into a glass and fill with orange juice. Stir. Serve as a float drink. Can also be mixed in a blender and served as a shake.
Developed by Orchid Lounge, NYC.

MALIBU COCONUT REFRESHER

2 parts Malibu coconut rum
2 parts lemon-lime soda
1 part lime juice

Serve over ice in a tall glass.
Developed by 40C, New York.

MALIBU ENDLESS SUMMER

2 parts Malibu Tropical banana rum
1 lemon wedge
1 lime wedge
banana slices for garnish

Crush lemons and limes. Add Malibu Tropical banana rum. Shake and strain into a martini glass. Garnish with banana slices.
Developed by Zombie Hut, NYC.

MALIBU FRENCH KICK

1 part Malibu passion fruit rum
splash Martell cognac
splash lemon juice
splash simple syrup

Developed by Sapa, New York.

MALIBU ISLA VIRGEN

2 parts Malibu coconut rum
½ part peach liquor
½ part amaretto

MALIBU MANGO BAY BREEZE

2 parts Malibu mango rum
1½ parts cranberry juice
1½ parts pineapple juice

MALIBU MANGO KAMIKAZE

1 part Malibu mango rum
1 part Stoli citrus vodka
½ part triple sec
¾ part fresh lime juice

MALIBU MANGO-LIME MARTINI

1½ parts Malibu mango rum
1½ parts Stoli Vanil vodka
1 part lime juice
1 part simple syrup

Developed by Sapa, New York

MALIBU MANGO MAI TAI

2 parts Malibu mango rum
1 part orange juice
1 part pineapple juice
splash lime juice
splash simple syrup
¼ oz. dark rum

*Pour first five ingredients into a glass and carefully float dark rum on top.
Developed by Sapa, New York.*

MALIBU MARGARITA

1¼ parts Malibu coconut rum
1 part Tezon tequila
½ part blue curaçao
½ part fresh lime juice
1½ part sweetened lemon juice

*Shake contents in an iced mixing glass and strain into an iced house
specialty glass. Garnish with a lime wedge.*

MALIBU MEGA-NUT

2 parts Malibu coconut rum
dash hazelnut liqueur
lemon-lime soda
shaved coconut flakes for garnish

Pour first two ingredients into a tall glass with ice and fill with lemon-lime soda. Garnish with shaved coconut flakes.
    Developed by Bamboo 52, New York.

MALIBU MEXICANA MAMA

1 part Malibu coconut rum
½ part Kahlúa coffee liqueur
½ part white crème de menthe
1½ parts heavy cream

Shake with ice and strain into a glass over crushed ice. Garnish with 2 mint leaves.
    Developed by 40C, New York.

MALIBU MIDNIGHT BREEZE

1 part Malibu coconut rum
½ part Malibu Tropical banana rum
1 part blue curaçao
pineapple juice to fill

Build with ice. Can be left shaken or layered.
    Developed by Orchid Lounge, New York.

MALIBU NOCHE LIBRE

1 part Malibu coconut rum
3 parts cola
splash lime juice
lime wedge for garnish

Serve in a Collins glass. Garnish with lime wedge.

MALIBU ON THE BEACH

1 oz. Malibu rum
½ oz. Baileys Irish cream

Serve as a shot.

MALIBU ORANGE COLADA

1½ oz. Malibu rum
1 oz. triple sec
4 oz. Coco Lopez real cream of coconut

MALIBU ORANGE PASSION

1 part Malibu passion fruit rum
1 part Stoli vodka
2 parts orange juice

Developed by Sapa, New York.

MALIBU PASSION FRUIT COSMO

1 part Malibu passion fruit rum
1 part Stoli Vanil vodka
1 part tonic water
splash cranberry juice

Developed by Sapa, New York.

MALIBU PASSION FRUIT SAKE-TINI

1 part Malibu passion fruit rum
1 part Stoli vodka
½ part sake
splash passion fruit puree

Developed by Sapa, New York.

MALIBU PASSION POPPER

1 part Malibu passion fruit rum
splash cola
splash cherry juice

Shake with ice and strain into a shot glass.
Developed by Bamboo 52, NY.

MALIBU PASSION TEA

1 part Malibu passion fruit rum
2 parts iced tea
1 part lemon-lime soda
lime slice for garnish

Serve over ice in a tall glass. Garnish with lime slice.

MALIBU PINEAPPLE COSMOPOLITAN

1½ parts Malibu pineapple rum
¾ part Hiram Walker triple sec
¾ part fresh lime juice
¾ part cranberry juice
lime wedge for garnish

Shake in an iced mixing glass and strain into a chilled cocktail glass. Garnish with lime wedge.

MALIBU PINEAPPLE SOURBALL

2 parts Malibu pineapple rum
splash cranberry juice
splash sour mix

Developed by Bamboo 52, NY.

MALIBU PINEAPPLEEZE

2 parts Malibu pineapple rum
2 parts pineapple juice
sour mix to fill
pineapple wedge for garnish

Pour first two ingredients into a tall glass and fill with sour mix. Garnish with pineapple wedge.
Developed by Bamboo 52, NY.

MALIBU PINEAPPLETINI

2 parts Malibu pineapple rum
½ part triple sec
dash lime juice
splash orange juice
orange slice for garnish

Shake with ice and strain into a martini glass. Garnish with an orange slice.
Developed by Bamboo 52, NY.

MALIBU RUM-BALL

2 parts Malibu coconut rum
2 parts melon liqueur or melon puree

Developed by Bamboo 52, NYC.

MALIBU SOL

3 parts Malibu coconut rum
½ part amaretto
½ part pineapple
½ part fresh lemon juice

Serve over ice in a rocks glass.

MALIBU SUMMER RAIN

1 part Malibu coconut rum
1 part Stoli vodka
1 part fresh lime juice
2 parts club soda
lime slice for garnish

Serve over ice in a tall glass and garnish with lime slice.

MALIBU SUNTAN

1½ oz. Malibu rum
5 oz. ice tea
lemon squeeze

Serve over ice.

MALIBU SWEET SIN

1 part Malibu mango rum
splash lime juice
splash cranberry juice
splash Bacardi 151 rum

Developed by Sapa, New York.

MALIBU TEQUILA BANANA

1 part Malibu Tropical banana rum
1 part Tezón Reposado tequila
splash lime juice

Developed by Orchid Lounge, NYC.

MALIBU TROPICAL BANANA SEX-A-PEEL

1 part Malibu Tropical banana rum
½ part Frangelico
½ part Irish cream
cherry for garnish

*Shake and serve on the rocks. Garnish with cherry.
Developed by Happy Ending Bar, NYC.*

MALIBU TROPICAL BREEZE

1 part Malibu coconut rum
1 part cranberry juice
2 parts pineapple juice
pineapple wedge for garnish

Serve in a tall glass and garnish with a pineapple wedge.

MALIBU TROPICAL EXPLOSION

2 parts Malibu coconut rum
2 parts pineapple juice
1 part pomegranate juice

Serve over ice in a tall glass.
    Developed by Orchid Lounge, New York.

MALIBU TROPICAL OASIS

2 parts Malibu coconut rum
1 part amaretto
2 parts frozen vanilla yogurt
1 part orange juice
1 part pineapple juice
dash honey

Blend and serve as a frozen shake.
    Developed by Orchid Lounge, New York.

MALIBU TROPICAL SANGRIA

2 parts Malibu Tropical banana rum
2 parts red wine
1 part 7UP
1 part orange juice
fresh fruit for garnish
cherry for garnish

Garnish with fresh fruits and cherry.
Developed by Orchid Lounge, New York.

MALIBU TROPICAL SOUR

1¼ parts Malibu Tropical banana rum
¾ part Hiram Walker sour apple
¾ part fresh sour mix
orange corkscrew for garnish

Shake and strain into a martini glass. Garnish with orange corkscrew.

MALIBU TROPICAL SUNRISE

1½ parts Malibu Tropical banana rum
1 part orange juice
1 part lemon-lime soda
cherry for garnish

Garnish with cherry.
Developed by Orchid Lounge, New York.

MALIBU VANILLA BANANA-TINI

1½ parts Malibu Tropical banana rum
2½ parts Stoli Vanil vodka
splash amaretto
orange twist for garnish

Garnish with orange twist.
Developed by Orchid Lounge, New York.

MALIBU VANILLA DREAM

1 part Malibu coconut rum
½ part Stoli Vanil vodka
½ part pineapple juice

Developed by 40C, New York.

MAMA WANA

1 oz. Cruzan orange rum
1 oz. Cruzan banana rum

Pour into a glass over chunky ice.

MAMBO KING

1 oz. Tommy Bahama White Sand rum
1 oz. coconut rum
½ oz. Tommy Bahama Golden Sun rum
½ oz. banana liqueur
3 oz. pineapple juice
pineapple spear for garnish

Shake in a pilsner glass with ice. Garnish with pineapple spear.

MAN EATER

1 oz. Whaler's Great White rum
4 oz. cola
½ oz. grenadine
cherry for garnish

Pour into a cocktail glass over ice. Garnish with cherry.

MANGO BAJITO

1 oz. Captain Morgan spiced rum
½ oz. triple sec
3 oz. mango juice
splash champagne

*Blend well with crushed ice. Serve in a cocktail or frappé glass.
    From the Ajili Mojili Restaurant.*

MANGO (OR GUAVA) DAIQUIRI

1½ oz. One Barrel rum
½ oz. fresh-squeezed lime juice
¼ oz. simple syrup
¾ oz. mango nectar (or guava nectar)
1 tsp. sugar
lime wedge for garnish

Shake with ice and strain into a chilled martini glass. Garnish with lime wedge.

MANGO FROZEN DREAM

1¼ oz. Captain Morgan Parrot Bay mango rum
½ oz. amaretto
½ oz. triple sec
2 oz. orange juice
1 scoop vanilla ice cream
orange wheel for garnish

Blend until smooth with 1 cup ice and pour into a glass. Garnish with orange wheel.

MANGO MADRAS

1½ oz. Parrot Bay mango rum
2 oz. cranberry juice
2 oz. orange juice
orange wedge for garnish

Pour into a glass over ice and stir. Garnish with orange wedge.

MANGO MAI TAI

1¼ oz. Captain Morgan Parrot Bay mango rum
1½ oz. margarita mix
1½ oz. pineapple juice
¼ oz. orgeat syrup
¼ oz. grenadine
pineapple slice for garnish
stemmed cherry for garnish

Shake with ice and pour into a glass. Garnish with pineapple slice and stemmed cherry.

MANGO MAMBO

1½ oz. Hiram Walker mango schnapps
1½ oz. Malibu Tropical banana rum

Shake with ice. Serve straight up in a chilled martini glass.

MANGO SPARKLER

¾ oz. One Barrel rum
¾ oz. mango nectar
2 oz. Moët nectar champagne

Stir with ice and strain into a chilled champagne flute.

MARTI MOJO

1 part Marti Autentico rum
1 part pineapple juice
1 part cranberry juice
mint sprig for garnish
pineapple for garnish

Shake well and serve in a martini glass. Garnish with fresh mint sprig and pineapple.

MARY PICKFORD

1½ oz. Puerto Rican white rum
1½ oz. pineapple juice
splash grenadine

Shake with 1 scoop crushed ice.

MIAMI SPECIAL

1 oz. Bacardi light rum
¼ oz. Hiram Walker white créme de menthe
¾ oz. lemon juice or Rose's lime juice

Shake and pour into a chilled martini glass.

MILLIONAIRE

¾ oz. Captain Morgan Original spiced rum
½ oz. créme de banana liqueur
2 oz. orange juice
1 oz. sour mix
½ oz. bar syrup
½ oz. grenadine

Blend first five ingredients with 1 cup crushed ice until slushy. Add grenadine and stir slightly.

THE MILLIONAIRE AND HIS WIFE

1 oz. Malibu mango rum
1 oz. Alize Red Passion liqueur
champagne
lemon twist for garnish

Shake first two ingredients with ice and strain into a martini glass. Top with champagne and garnish with a twist of lemon.
    Developed by Happy Endings, New York.

MISSION MADNESS

2 oz. Whaler's Vanille rum
¾ oz. amaretto
2 oz. passion fruit juice
2 oz. orange juice
lime slice for garnish
cherry for garnish

Fill hurricane glass with ice. Add ingredients into cocktail shaker and mix well. Pour over ice and garnish with lime slice and cherry.

MO BAY MARTINI

2 oz. Appleton Estate V/X Jamaica rum
¼ oz. extra dry vermouth
olive for garnish

Shake with ice and strain into a martini glass. Garnish with olive.

MOJITO (267 SIGNATURE MANGO)

2½ oz. 267 Infusion mango rum
4 fresh mint sprigs (plus more for garnish)
splash soda water
lime wedge for garnish

Muddle four fresh mint sprigs at the bottom of a glass. Add Infusion mango rum with a splash of soda water. Garnish with lime wedge and more mint sprigs.

MOJITO (APPLE PEAR)

1 part Bacardi Limón
1 part Bacardi Big Apple
2 mint leaves
2 parts pineapple juice
2 parts club soda
2 lime wedges
1 tbsp. sugar

Mix sugar, mint leaves, and lime in a glass and crush well. Add Bacardi Limón, Bacardi Big Apple, and pineapple juice, then top off with club soda.

MOJITO (BEE)

1 part Bacardi Rum
3 parts club soda
12 mint leaves
juice of ½ lime
1 tbsp. honey
mint sprigs or lime wheel for garnish

Place mint leaves and crushed ice in a glass. Muddle well with a pestle. Add lime juice, honey, and Bacardi; stir well. Top off with club soda, stir, and garnish with sprigs of mint or a lime wheel.

MOJITO (BERMUDA GOLD)

2 oz. Gosling's Gold Bermuda rum
6–8 spearmint leaves
¼ oz. fresh lime juice
1 tsp. superfine sugar
½ oz. club soda
¼ oz. Gosling's Black Seal rum

In a large old-fashioned glass, muddle the lime juice, sugar, and spearmint leaves (save a couple for garnish), bruising the spearmint well. Add Gosling's Gold Bermuda rum and ice. Top with a splash of club soda and a float of Gosling's Black Seal rum. Garnish with remaining spearmint leaves.

MOJITO (BIG APPLE)

1 part Bacardi Big Apple rum
3 parts club soda
12 mint leaves
½ lime
½ part sugar
mint sprigs, lime wheel, or green apple slices for garnish

Place mint leaves, sugar, and lime in a glass. Crush well with a pestle. Add Bacardi Big Apple rum, top off with club soda, stir well, and garnish with sprigs of mint and a lime wheel or green apple slice.

MOJITO (BRINLEY LIME)

2 parts Brinley Gold lime rum
3 parts club soda
½ lime
6 mint leaves
1 tsp. sugar

Squeeze in and muddle ½ lime. Blend with crushed ice.

MOJITO (COCO RUM)

1 part Bacardi Coco rum
3 parts lemon-lime soda
12 mint leaves
½ lime
mint sprigs for garnish

Place mint leaves and lime in glass and crush well. Add rum and soda and garnish with sprigs of mint.

MOJITO (CUCUMBER)

1½ oz. 10 Cane rum
1 oz. fresh-squeezed lime juice
1 oz. simple syrup
8–10 mint leaves
4 pieces peeled cucumber
club soda to top
cucumber slice/stick for garnish

Place simple syrup, mint leaves, and cucumber in the bottom of a tall glass. Press gently with a muddler. Fill with cracked ice. Add 10 Cane and lime juice. Stir gently and top off with soda. Garnish with a slice or stick of cucumber.
    Listed on 28 Degrees cocktail menu in Boston.

MOJITO (GINGER)

1 part Bacardi rum
3 parts ginger beer
12 mint leaves
½ lime
½ part simple sugar

Same as Original Bacardi Mojito, but using ginger beer rather than club soda.

MOJITO (GRAND MELON)

1 part Bacardi Grand Melon rum
3 parts club soda
12 mint leaves
½ lime
½ part sugar
mint sprigs for garnish
lime wheel or watermelon slice for garnish

Place mint leaves, sugar, and lime in a glass. Crush well with a pestle. Add Bacardi Grand Melon rum, top off with club soda, stir well, and garnish with sprigs of mint and a lime wheel or watermelon slice.

MOJITO (LIMÓN RUM)

1 part Bacardi Limón rum
3 parts club soda
12 mint leaves
½ lime
½ part sugar
mint sprigs for garnish
lime or lemon wheel for garnish

Place mint leaves, sugar, and lime in a glass. Crush well with a pestle. Add Bacardi Limón rum, top off with club soda, stir well and garnish with sprigs of mint and a lime or lemon wheel.

MOJITO (LOW CAL BACARDI)

1 part Bacardi rum
3 parts club soda
12 mint leaves
½ lime
3 packets Splenda
mint sprigs for garnish
lime wedge for garnish

Place mint leaves, Splenda, and lime in glass. Muddle with pestle. Add Bacardi, then club soda. Stir well and garnish with mint sprigs and a lime wedge.

MOJITO (MALIBU MANGO)

2½ parts Malibu mango rum
½ part fresh lime juice
½ part simple syrup
3–4 mint sprigs (plus extra for garnish)
3 lime wedges (plus 1 for garnish)
2–3 splashes club soda

Pour lime juice and simple syrup into a glass. Add mint sprigs and lime wedges, and muddle contents thoroughly. Add ice, Malibu mango rum, and splashes of club soda. Garnish with a lime wedge and mint sprigs.

MOJITO (MALIBU PASSION FRUIT)

2 parts Malibu passion fruit rum
3 tbsp. fresh lemon juice
2 tbsp. sugar
club soda
fresh mint

Developed by Sapa, New York.

MOJITO (MILLIONAIRE)

1½ oz. 10 Cane rum
½ oz. simple syrup
1 oz. fresh-squeezed lime juice
8–10 mint leaves
splash Moët & Chandon champagne
mint sprig for garnish

Place simple syrup and mint leaves in the bottom of a tall glass. Press gently with a muddler. Fill with cracked ice. Add 10 Cane and lime juice. Stir gently and top off with Moët & Chandon champagne. Garnish with a mint sprig.

MOJITO (MALIBU NOCHE BLANCA)

3 parts Malibu coconut rum
1 part fresh lime juice
1 part simple syrup
1 part club soda
8 mint leaves
lime wheel for garnish

Serve in a Collins glass. Garnish with a lime wheel.

MOJITO (O)

1 part Bacardi O rum
3 parts club soda
12 mint leaves
½ lime
½ part sugar
mint sprigs for garnish
lime or orange wheel for garnish

Place mint leaves, sugar, and lime in a glass. Muddle well with a pestle. Add Bacardi O rum, top off with club soda, stir well, and garnish with sprigs of mint and a lime or orange wheel.

MOJITO (ORIGINAL BACARDI)

1 part Bacardi rum
3 parts club soda
12 mint leaves
½ lime
½ part sugar
mint sprigs or lime wheel for garnish

Place mint leaves, sugar, and lime in a glass. Muddle well with a pestle. Add Bacardi, top off with club soda, stir well, and garnish with sprigs of mint or a lime wheel.

MOJITO (PEACH RED RUM)

1 part Bacardi Peach Red rum
3 parts club soda
12 mint leaves
½ peach
½ part sugar
mint sprigs for garnish
peach slice for garnish

Place mint leaves, sugar, and peach in a glass. Crush well with a pestle. Add Bacardi Peach Red rum, top off with club soda, stir well, and garnish with sprigs of mint and a peach slice.

MOJITO (SONNY'S)

½ lime, cut into wedges
2 tbsp. sugar
½ oz. Chateaux peppermint schnapps
1 oz. Bacardi Superior rum
ice
club soda to top
lime wheel for garnish

Muddle lime and sugar in the bottom of an 8-oz. glass. Add schnapps, ice, and Bacardi. Top with club soda and garnish with lime wheel.

MOJITO (SPICY)

1½ oz. Flor de Cana 4-year-old extra-dry rum
2 1-inch cubes watermelon
1 slice jalapeño
10 fresh mint leaves
¾ oz. fresh lime juice
½ oz. simple syrup
1½ oz. club soda
watermelon triangle for garnish
jalapeño slice for garnish
mint sprig for garnish

In a mixing glass, add jalapeno slice followed by watermelon cubes. Muddle with mint. Add Flor de Cana 4-year-old extra-dry rum, simple syrup, and lime juice. Add ice and shake. Strain over fresh ice into a highball glass and top with club soda. Integrate club soda with bar spoon. Garnish with watermelon triangle, slice of jalapeño, and mint sprig.

MOJITO (TRADITIONAL/CUBAN)

1 oz. Bacardi light rum
1 tbsp. sugar
1 tbsp. lime juice
6-inch sprig of mint
ice to fill
3 oz. club soda
2 dashes Angostura bitters

Place sugar, lime juice, and mint in a Collins glass. Crush mint stalk with pestle and muddle with juice and sugar. Add rum, add ice to top of glass, and top off with club soda and bitters. Stir well. Enjoy!

MOJITO (WATER CLUB)

1½ oz. Bacardi light rum
½ oz. fresh-squeezed lemon juice
½ oz. fresh-squeezed lime juice
1 oz. Guarapo (sugar cane extract)
½ oz. blue curacao
6 mint leaves
splash club soda
fresh mint for garnish

Shake well with ice. Serve in a Collins glass and garnish with fresh mint. From the Water Club Hotel.

MOJITO (WILD BERRY)

1½ oz. Pyrat XO Reserve rum
2–3 each fresh blackberries, blueberries, and raspberries
12–14 fresh mint leaves
juice of 1 lime
1 oz. simple syrup
spritz soda water
mint sprig for garnish
powdered sugar for garnish

Muddle mint, simple syrup, wild berries, and lime juice in a 14-oz. high-ball glass. Fill glass with crushed ice, then add Pyrat XO Reserve rum. Stir well until the ice is reduced by ⅓, then top with more crushed ice, stirring until glass begins to frost on the outside. Spritz with soda water and stir one last time to incorporate. Garnish with two long straws and a mint sprig that has been dusted with powdered sugar.

MOJITO (WINTER)

1½ oz. Ron Anejo Pampero Especial rum
¾ oz. fresh lemon juice
¼ oz. maple syrup
2 dashes Angostura bitters
6 sprigs mint

Muddle 5 mint sprigs and bitters in a shaker. Add Ron Anejo Pampero Especial rum, lime, and maple syrup. Let sit for 1 minute. Shake hard. Strain into a double old-fashioned glass over fresh ice. Garnish with remaining mint sprig. If made with hot water, it becomes a toddy.

MOJITO MARTINI

1½ oz. Bacardi Limón
½ oz. lemon vodka
½ lime, quartered
8 mint leaves

Fill martini glass with crushed ice to chill. Fill a shaker half full with crushed ice. Add the rest of the ingredients, cover, and shake for about 1 minute. Remove ice from glass and pour in the mojito.

MOM'S SANGRIA

8 Red Delicious apple slices
2 small oranges cut into thin quarters
12 strawberries, sliced
2 lemons cut in thin slices
12 oz. freshly squeezed orange juice
12 oz. fresh lemon juice
6 oz. simple syrup
2 cinnamon sticks
8 oz. Pyrat XO Reserve rum
8 oz. Citronge
2 bottles of Spanish red wine
7UP to top

Place above ingredients, excluding 7UP, into a large glass container. Cover and refrigerate overnight. When ready to serve, pour into a pitcher over ice, filling ⅔ of the way. Add fresh sliced fruits and top with 7UP. Stir gently to mix. Serve in wine glasses over ice.

MONKEY SPECIAL

1 oz. dark rum
1 oz. light rum
½ oz. banana, peeled
2 oz. vanilla/chocolate ice cream
shaved chocolate for garnish

Sprinkle with shaved chocolate.

MONKEY WRENCH

1½ oz. Sailor Jerry Spiced Navy rum
grapefruit juice to fill

Pour Sailor Jerry Spiced Navy rum over ice in a Collins glass. Fill with grapefruit juice and stir.

MONTEGO MARGARITA

1½ oz. Appleton Estate V/X rum
½ oz. triple sec
2 oz. lemon or lime juice
1 scoop crushed ice

Blend. Serve in a tall glass.

MOONLIGHT SAIL

1 oz. Admiral Nelson's raspberry rum
1 oz. Admiral Nelson's coconut rum
1 oz. vodka
1 oz. Arrow sloe gin
½ oz. amaretto
2 oz. orange juice
3 oz. pineapple juice
cherry for garnish
lemon twist for garnish

Shake well and pour into a tall glass over ice. Garnish with cherry and lemon twist.

THE MORGAN CANNONBALL

1¼ oz. Captain Morgan Original Spiced rum
3 oz. pineapple juice
white crème de menthe to float

Blend first two ingredients with ice. Float white crème de menthe. Serve in a tall glass.

MORGAN'S JOLLY ROGER

¾ oz. Captain Morgan Original spiced rum
¾ oz. cinnamon schnapps

Serve as a shot.

MORGAN'S RED ROUGE

1 oz. Captain Morgan Original spiced rum
½ oz. blackberry brandy
2 oz. pineapple juice
½ oz. lemon juice

Stir.

MORGAN'S SPICED RUM ALEXANDER

1 oz. Captain Morgan Original spiced rum
½ oz. créme de cacao
1 oz. heavy cream
grated nutmeg for dusting

Shake and strain into a glass. Dust with nutmeg.

MORGAN'S WENCH

¾ oz. Captain Morgan Original spiced rum
¾ oz. amaretto
dark crème de cacao to float

Serve as a shot.

THE MOUNT GAY GRINDER

1½ oz. Mount Gay rum
cranberry juice to fill
splash 7UP

Serve in a tall glass.

MR. LICK

1 oz. Gosling's Black Seal rum
1 oz. apricot liqueur
pineapple juice to fill
splash grenadine

Shake over ice and serve on the rocks.

MTB & GINGER

1½ parts Malibu Tropical banana rum
ginger ale
lemon slice for garnish

Garnish with lemon slice.
Developed by 40C, NYC.

MUFFLED SCREECH

1 oz. Newfoundland Screech rum
¼ oz. triple sec or Grand Marnier
2 oz. cream or milk

Layer Newfoundland Screech and triple sec or Grand Marnier over a few ice cubes in a glass. Top with cream or milk. No one can hear you scream . . .

MYERS'S APPLESAUCE

1½ shot Myers's rum
1 orange slice
6 oz. hot cider

Stir in a heat-proof mug.

MYERS'S HEAT WAVE

¾ oz. Myers's Original dark rum
½ oz. peach schnapps
6 oz. pineapple juice
1 splash grenadine

Pour first two ingredients into a glass over ice. Fill with juice and top with grenadine.

MYERS'S HONEY POT

2 oz. Myers's rum
1 tbsp. honey
6 oz. hot water
pinch grated nutmeg

In the bottom of a heat-proof mug, stir honey and Myers's rum until honey is dissolved. Fill with hot water. Stir until blended. Sprinkle with nutmeg. If desired, molasses can be substituted for honey.

MYERS'S LEMON DROP

1 shot Myers's rum
2–3 lumps sugar
juice of ½ lemon
6 oz. hot water
1 cinnamon stick

In a heat-proof mug, muddle sugar, Myers's rum, and lemon juice until sugar is dissolved. Add hot water. Stir with a cinnamon stick until well blended.

MYERS'S LOUNGE LIZARD

1 oz. Myers's rum
½ oz. Leroux amaretto
cola to fill
lime wedge for garnish

Mix first two ingredients in a tall glass over ice. Fill with cola. Garnish with lime wedge.

MYERS'S RUM AND TROPICAL HOT COCOA

16 oz. Myers's rum
4 oz. bittersweet hot chocolate
chocolate-covered strawberry for garnish

Pour into a mug and top with shaved bittersweet chocolate curls. Garnish with chocolate-covered strawberry.

MYERS'S RUM BARREL

1 shot Myers's rum
8 oz. hot cola-flavored beverage
lemon slice for garnish

Gently stir in a heat-proof glass or mug. Garnish with lemon slice.

MYERS'S RUM COZY

2 oz. Myers's rum
1 tsp. sugar
6 oz. hot tea
½ oz. triple sec
dash nutmeg

Stir first four ingredients in a heat-proof mug. Sprinkle with nutmeg.

MYERS'S RUM HOLIDAY GROG

1 oz. Myers's rum
4 oz. fresh apple cider, hot
thinly-sliced lemon and orange wheels studded with cloves for
    garnish

Pour into a mug. Garnish with lemon and orange wheels.

MYERS'S RUM HOLIDAY NOG

4 oz. Myers's rum
1 pint melted low-fat vanilla ice cream
maraschino cherries for garnish
mint sprigs for garnish

*Mix in a large bowl and chill. Pour into champagne flutes and garnish
each with a maraschino cherry and a fresh mint sprig. Serves 6 to 8.*

MYERS'S RUM PLANTER'S PUNCH

1¼ oz. Myers's rum
3 oz. orange juice
juice of ? lemon or lime
1 tsp. superfine sugar
dash grenadine
orange slice for garnish
maraschino cherry for garnish

*Shake or blend until frothy. Serve over shaved ice in a highball glass.
Garnish with orange slice and maraschino cherry.*

MYERS'S RUM SHARKBITE

1¼ oz. Myers's rum
orange juice to fill
splash Rose's grenadine

Pour Myers's rum into a tumbler over ice cubes. Fill with orange juice and add a splash of Rose's grenadine.

MYERS'S RUM SUNSHINE COCKTAIL

1¼ oz. Myers's rum
2 oz. orange juice
2 oz. grapefruit juice
½ tsp. superfine sugar
dash Angostura bitters
cherry for garnish

Shake with ice until frothy and strain into a highball glass over shaved ice. Garnish with cherry.

MYERS'S SIZZLER

1 shot Myers's rum
1 tbsp. powdered cocoa
1 tbsp. sugar
1 cup scalded milk
sweetened whipped cream to top
instant coffee or powdered cocoa for sprinkling

In a heat-proof mug, stir cocoa and sugar. Add hot milk and Myers's rum. Stir until cocoa is dissolved. Top with whipped cream and sprinkle with instant coffee or cocoa.

MYRTLE BANK PUNCH

1¼ oz. Captain Morgan Original spiced rum
¼ oz. grenadine
1 oz. lime juice
1 tsp. sugar
¼ oz. cherry liqueur
cherry for garnish
orange wedge for garnish

Pour first four ingredients into a 10-oz. glass over crushed ice. Top with cherry liqueur and garnish with cherry and orange wedge.

NAVY GROG

½ oz. Sailor Jerry Spiced Navy rum
½ oz. vodka
½ oz. tequila
½ oz. triple sec
1 oz. amaretto
1 oz. orange juice
1 oz. pineapple juice
1 oz. cranberry juice
orange slice for garnish
cherry for garnish

Mix with ice and pour into a hurricane glass. Garnish with orange slice and cherry.

NEON

5 oz. Captain Morgan Parrot Bay coconut rum
1 oz. Black Haus blackberry schnapps
3 oz. pineapple juice

Serve over ice.

NEWFOUNDLAND NIGHT-CAP

1¼ oz. Newfoundland Screech rum
1–2 tsp. brown sugar
coffee to fill
whipped cream to top

Pour first two ingredients into a coffee cup. Fill with coffee and stir. Top with whipped cream. Take this one to bed with you!

NILLA COLA

1 oz. Whaler's Vanille rum
5 oz. cola
lime squeeze
lime wedge for garnish

Pour into a cocktail glass over ice. Garnish with lime wedge.

NINETINI

1 oz. Angostura 1919 Premium rum
½ oz. orange curacao
2 oz. sweet and sour mix
½ tsp. sugar
4 dashes Angostura aromatic bitters

Shake.

NUFF RUM

2 oz. Wray & Nephew rum
3 oz. Stones ginger wine
½ oz. Limoncello
½ oz. peach syrup
3 dashes Angostura bitters
fresh apple juice to float
orange peel for garnish
lemon peel for garnish

Build in an old-fashioned glass over cubed ice and stir. Garnish with orange and lemon peel.

NYOTA (SWAHILI FOR *STAR*)

3 oz. Starr African rum
1½ oz. acerola puree
Llopart Rosa Cava champagne
yellow cherry for garnish

Shake first two ingredients with ice and strain into a martini glass. Top off with Llopart Rosa Cava or other champagne. Garnish with yellow cherry.

THE OLD BERMUDIAN

1½ oz. Gosling's Gold Bermuda rum
6 mint leaves
2 dashes bitters
½ oz. lime juice
½ oz. simple syrup
¼ oz. champagne
lime twist for garnish

Muddle mint leaves in a shaker half filled with ice. Add Gosling's rum, bitters, lime juice, and simple syrup. Shake well and pour into a Collins glass. Top with champagne. Garnish with lime twist.
Created by Tom Colicchio, Craft Restaurant.

"ONE-GRAND" COCKTAIL

1½ oz. One Barrel rum
½ oz. Grand Marnier
½ oz. mango nectar
¼ oz. fresh-squeezed lime juice
mango slice for garnish

Shake with ice and strain into a chilled martini glass. Garnish with a mango slice.

ORANGE BOWL

1 oz. Bacardi O rum
4 oz. orange juice
2 oz. ginger ale
1 oz. Bacardi Select rum
orange slice for garnish
cinnamon stick for garnish

Pour first four ingredients into a wine glass. Float Bacardi Select rum on top. Garnish with orange slice and cinnamon stick.
   From the Pikayo Restaurant.

ORANGE COLADA

2 oz. Cruzan orange rum
1 15-oz. can Coco Lopez real cream of coconut
4 oz. pineapple juice
4 oz. orange juice

Blend with 4 cups of ice.

ORIGINAL PIÑA COLADA

2 oz. Puerto Rican light rum (or, for a different twist, try Captain
   Morgan Parrot Bay coconut rum)
1 oz. Coco Lopez real cream of coconut
1 oz. heavy cream
6 oz. fresh pineapple juice
pineapple wedge for garnish
maraschino cherry for garnish

*Blend for 15 seconds with ½ cup crushed ice. Pour into a 12-oz. glass.
Garnish with pineapple wedge and maraschino cherry. Add a red straw.
Tip: For the best tropical taste, always use fresh pineapple juice, never
canned or mixes.*
   Caribe Hilton Hotel

ORO & SODA

2 oz. Oronoco rum
splash soda
lime wedge for garnish

*Pour Oronoco rum into a rocks glass over ice. Splash with soda and stir.
Garnish with lime wedge.*

ORO COSMO

2 oz. Oronoco rum
1 tbsp. Grand Marnier
1 tbsp. cranberry juice
1 tbsp. lime juice
lime twist for garnish

Shake over ice and strain into a chilled martini glass. Garnish with lime twist.

ORO GIMLET

2 oz. Oronoco rum
2 wedges lime
2 oz. lime juice
splash tonic
splash soda
dash simple syrup
lime wedge for garnish

Muddle lime wedges in a shaker. Add Oronoco rum, lime juice, and simple syrup, and shake vigorously with crushed ice. Strain into a Collins glass over ice cubes. Top with equal splashes tonic and soda. Garnish with lime wedge.

ORO ON THE ROCKS

2 oz. Oronoco rum
lime slice for garnish

Pour Oronoco into a short rocks glass over ice cubes. Garnish with a freshly cut lime slice.

THE OTHER WOMAN

1 oz. Admiral Nelson's Premium vanilla rum
1 oz. white soda
splash cola
cherry for garnish

Pour into a cocktail glass and garnish with cherry.

PAINKILLER

2, 3, or 4 parts Pusser's rum—your choice!
4 parts pineapple juice
1 part cream of coconut
1 part orange juice
grated nutmeg for garnish

Serve on the rocks with a generous amount of fresh nutmeg on top.

PARISIAN BLONDE

1½ oz. Bacardi light rum
¾ oz. cream
½ oz. orange curaçao
maraschino cherry for garnish

Garnish with maraschino cherry.

PARROT BAY MANGO MADNESS

1½ oz. Captain Morgan Parrot Bay mango rum
2 oz. cranberry juice
2 oz. orange juice

Shake with ice and pour into a glass.

PARROT PASSION

2 oz. Bacardi Limón rum
½ oz. Cointreau
3 oz. orange juice
3 oz. passion fruit juice
orange slice for garnish
pineapple chunk for garnish

Blend with ice and served in a chilled martini glass. Garnish with a slice of orange and a chunk of pineapple.
   From the Parrot Club Restaurant.

PASSION FRUIT DAIQUIRI (BRUNCH COCKTAIL)

2 oz. 10 Cane rum
1 oz. fresh-squeezed lime juice
1 oz. simple syrup
1 oz. passion fruit puree
lime wheel for garnish

Combine all ingredients in a mixing glass. Add ice and shake vigorously. Strain into a chilled cocktail glass. Garnish with lime wheel.
   Created by the Movida Group.

PASSION OF BELIZE

¾ oz. One Barrel rum
¾ oz. passion fruit nectar
2 oz. Moët nectar champagne
1 tsp. fresh passion fruit (1 passion fruit, cut in half and spooned out)

Stir with ice and strain into a chilled champagne flute.

PASSIONPOLITAN

1 oz. Parrot Bay passion fruit rum
¼ oz. triple sec
2 oz. cranberry juice
1 squirt lime juice
lime wedge for garnish

Pour into a glass over ice and stir. Garnish with lime wedge.

THE PATIO

1 oz. Bacardi O rum
½ oz. triple sec
2 oz. lemonade
pinch superfine sugar
3 mint leaves
soda water to top

Shake first four ingredients with ice and pour into a highball glass. Add mint leaves and top with soda water.

PAULISTANO

1½ oz. Oronoco rum
3 wedges lime
2 mint leaves
3 oz. pressed pineapple juice
mint sprig for garnish

In a shaker, muddle mint leaves and lime wedges. Add Oronoco rum and pineapple juice; shake with crushed ice. Pour into a glass and garnish with mint sprig.

PB BREEZE

1½ oz. Parrot Bay coconut rum
2 oz. cranberry juice
2 oz. pineapple juice
pineapple slice for garnish

Pour into a glass over ice and stir. Garnish with pineapple slice.

PEACH BANANA DAIQUIRI

1½ oz. Puerto Rican light rum
½ medium banana, diced
1 oz. fresh lime juice
¼ cup sliced peaches (fresh, frozen, or canned)

Blend with 1 cup crushed ice.

PEACH DAIQUIRI

1 oz. Captain Morgan Original spiced rum
¼ oz. peach schnapps
4 oz. frozen pureed peaches
3 oz. sour mix
peach slice for garnish
mint sprig for garnish

Blend with crushed ice to desired consistency. Garnish with peach slice and mint sprig.

PEACH MELBA

2 oz. Captain Morgan Original spiced rum
¾ oz. raspberry liqueur
2 oz. peach cocktail mix
2 peach halves (canned)
1 oz. heavy cream
raspberry syrup or fresh raspberries to top

Blend with 2 cups crushed ice until smooth and creamy. Serve in 16-oz. specialty glass. Top with raspberry syrup or fresh raspberries.

PEACH PUNCH

⅓ oz. Captain Morgan Original spiced rum
½ oz. peach schnapps
2 oz. piña colada mix
4 oz. orange juice
fresh peach for garnish

Blend with crushed ice until frozen. Garnish with fresh peach.

PEAR BLOSSOM

1½ oz. Tommy Bahama White Sand rum
1 oz. premium orange liqueur
1½ oz. pear juice
1 oz. sour mix

Shake at least 20 times with ice and strain into a chilled martini glass. Garnish with a fresh orchid.

PELICAN PUNCH

1½ oz. Admiral Nelson's raspberry rum
½ oz. dark rum
¼ oz. 151-proof rum
1½ oz. pineapple juice
1½ oz. orange juice
1 oz. sweet and sour
orange slice for garnish
lemon wheel for garnish

Build in a hurricane glass over ice. Garnish with orange slice and lemon wheel.

PIÑA COLADA MARTINI

2 oz. Cruzan pineapple rum, chilled
1 oz. Cruzan coconut rum
pineapple wedge for garnish

Mix in a martini glass. Garnish with fresh pineapple wedge.

PINEAPPLE SPLASH

¾ oz. Captain Morgan Parrot Bay pineapple rum
¾ oz. Captain Morgan Parrot Bay coconut rum
4 oz. orange juice

Pour into a glass over ice and stir.

PINEAPPLE TWIST

1½ oz. Appleton Estate V/X Jamaica rum
6 oz. pineapple juice
½ tsp. lemon juice

Shake and pour into a tall glass over ice.

PINEAPPLETON

1½ oz. Appleton Estate Extra Jamaica rum
6 oz. pineapple juice
fruit slice for garnish

Pour into a highball or Collins glass over ice. Garnish with desired fruit slice.

PINK LEMONADE

1¼ oz. Captain Morgan Original spiced rum
3 oz. cranberry juice
2 oz. club soda
juice of ¼ lemon
lemon twist for garnish

Build first two ingredients in a glass over ice. Top with club soda and lemon juice. Garnish with a lemon twist.

PINK ORCHID

1¼ oz. Captain Morgan Original spiced rum
2 oz. cranberry juice
2 oz. pineapple juice
¼ oz. cream of coconut
fresh mint for garnish

Blend with crushed ice. Garnish with fresh mint.

PINK PANTHER

1¼ oz. Bacardi light rum
¾ oz. lemon juice
¾ oz. cream
½ oz. Rose's grenadine

PINK PLANET

3 oz. 3-Star Rhum Barbancourt
2 tsp. lime or lemon juice
2 oz. white Dubonnet

Mix with ½ cup crushed ice and pour into a champagne glass.

PINKY & THE CAPTAIN

1¼ oz. Captain Morgan Original spiced rum
5 oz. grapefruit juice
pink grapefruit section or lime wheel for garnish

Pour into a highball glass over ice. Garnish with pink grapefruit section or lime wheel.

PIÑO FRIO

2 oz. Captain Morgan Original spiced rum
3 oz. (2 slices) pineapple
1 tsp. sugar
maraschino cherry or pineapple wedge for garnish

*Blend thoroughly with 1 cup crushed ice and pour into 14-oz. glass.
Garnish with maraschino cherry or pineapple wedge.*

PIRATE'S PUNCH

1¾ oz. Rhum Barbancourt
¼ oz. sweet vermouth
dash Angostura bitters

Shake.

PLANTER'S PUNCH

2 oz. Captain Morgan Original spiced rum
2 oz. orange juice
2 oz. pineapple juice
¼ oz. lime juice
¼ oz. lemon juice
1 tsp. bar sugar
dash grenadine
fruit slice for garnish

*Shake with ice and strain into a highball glass over ice. Garnish with
fruit slice.*

PLANTEUR

2 oz. white or dark Rhum de Martinique
4 oz. exotic fruit juice
⅛ oz. cane syrup
⅛ oz. cinnamon
⅛ oz. grated nutmeg
⅛ oz. vanilla
orange slice for garnish
maraschino cherry for garnish

Shake with ice. Serve on the rocks or straight up in a martini glass. Garnish with sliced orange and maraschino cherry.

PLUS H

1 oz. Bacardi O rum
1 oz. Bacardi Grand melon rum
1 oz. Malibu rum
pineapple juice to fill
splash ginger ale

Pour first three ingredients into a glass and fill with pineapple juice. Top with ginger ale.
From Sarah Tartaglia, Avenel, NJ.

POINCIANA

1 oz. light rum
2 maraschino cherries
1 oz. apple juice
½ oz. grenadine

Shake with ice. Serve on the rocks.

POMA-MAMA-BU

1½ parts Hiram Walker pomegranate schnapps
1½ parts Malibu Tropical banana

Shake with ice and strain into a chilled martini glass, or serve on the rocks.

PORT ROYAL

1½ oz. Appleton Estate V/X Jamaica rum
½ oz. sweet vermouth
juice of ¼ orange
juice of ¼ lime
orange or lime wedge for garnish

Shake with ice and strain into a large rocks glass over ice cubes. Garnish with orange or lime wedge.

PRESIDENTE

1½ oz. Puerto Rican white rum
¼ oz. dry vermouth
¾ oz. sweet vermouth
splash grenadine

Mix with 6–8 ice cubes.

PRINCESS MORGAN

¾ oz. Captain Morgan Original spiced rum
¼ oz. créme de banana
2½ oz. orange juice
2 oz. club soda

Pour the first three ingredients into a glass over ice. Stir. Add the soda and stir gently.

PROFESSOR & MARY ANNE

¾ part Malibu mango rum
¼ part Malibu banana rum
½ part pineapple juice

Developed by Happy Endings, New York.

PUERTO RICAN RUM CAPPUCCINO

1½ oz. Puerto Rican dark rum
1 tsp. sugar
Equal parts:
   hot strong coffee
   steamed milk
whipped cream to top
cinnamon to taste

Pour first two ingredients into a mug and add coffee and milk. Top with whipped cream and cinnamon.

PUMPKIN SPICE

1½ oz. Cruzan mango rum
1½ oz. pumpkin pie filling
1 oz. cream
¼ oz. Monin gingerbread syrup

Shake and strain through a sieve into a hollowed-out mini pumpkin.

PUNCH ISLANDS

2 tsp. sugar cane
2 oz. white Rhum Barbancourt
2 oz. pineapple juice
juice of ½ orange
juice of ½ lemon
soda to top
lemon wedge for garnish

Mix the pineapple juice and sugar cane, then add the orange and lemon juices. Pour into a glass and add white Rhum Barbancourt. Top with soda and mix with a spoon. To finish, add ice cubes and garnish with a wedge of lemon.

PURPLE DEW

1½ oz. Appleton Estate Extra Jamaica rum
3 oz. cranberry juice
1 oz. clear syrup
1 oz. blue curacao
1 oz. lime juice

Pour into a Collins or punch glass over ice.

PURPLE FLIRT

1 oz. Gosling's Black Seal rum
¼ oz. blue curacao
½ oz. sweet and sour
¼ oz. grenadine
1 oz. pineapple juice
orange slice or cherry for garnish

Shake and strain into a chilled rocks glass. Garnish with orange slice and cherry.

PYRAT PUNCH

2 oz. Pyrat XO Reserve rum
juice of ½ lime
dash bitters
2 oz. soda water
splash pineapple juice (optional)
splash grapefruit juice (optional)
¼ tsp. grated nutmeg
fresh cherries for garnish

Shake first three ingredients gently over ice. Pour into a margarita glass. Add pineapple and grapefruit juice if desired. Top with soda water. Garnish with nutmeg and fresh cherries.

PYRAT XO REFRESHER

2 oz. Pyrat XO Reserve rum
tonic to fill
lime wedge for garnish

Pour over ice into a bucket glass. Garnish with a squeezed lime wedge.

PYRAT'S SIN

½ oz. Pyrat Cask 23 rum
½ oz. Grand Marnier Cent Cinquantenaire
1 sugar cube soaked with two dashes Angostura bitters
chilled brut-style champagne to fill
lemon peel for garnish
strawberry slice for garnish

Place the sugar cube into a chilled champagne glass. Add Pyrat Cask 23 rum and Grand Mariner Cent Cinquantenaire. Fill with champagne. Garnish with lemon peel and strawberry slice.

QUARTER DECK

1 oz. Puerto Rican light rum
½ oz. Puerto Rican dark rum
½ oz. cream sherry
½ oz. lime juice

Shake.

QUEENS PARK SWIZZLE

1¼ oz. Captain Morgan Original spiced rum
juice of ½ large lime
½ oz. sweet and sour mix
½ oz. simple syrup
3 mint leaves

Squeeze lime and drop shell into 14-oz. glass. Add 1 mint leaf. Add shaved ice and remaining ingredients, except mint. Stir until glass is frosty. Garnish with remaining mint leaves.

R & B

1¼ oz. Captain Morgan Original spiced rum
2 oz. orange juice
2 oz. pineapple juice
splash grenadine

Pour into a glass over ice.

RACER'S EDGE

1 oz. Bacardi light rum
¼ oz. Hiram Walker green créme de menthe
grapefruit juice to fill

Pour Bacardi light rum into a tall glass half filled with ice. Fill with grape-fruit juice and float créme de menthe.

RASPBERRY COLADA

1½ oz. rum
1½ oz. Chambord
3 oz. pineapple juice
1 oz. Coco Lopez real cream of coconut

Blend. Serve in a tall glass.

RASPBERRY FROST

2 oz. light rum
1 oz. Chambord
2 oz. Coco Lopez real cream of coconut
dash lime juice
maraschino cherry for garnish

Blend first four ingredients. Garnish with maraschino cherry.

RASPBERRY LEMONADE

2 oz. Cruzan raspberry rum
2 oz. lemonade
lemon slice for garnish

Serve on the rocks. Garnish with lemon slice.

RED HAWAIIAN

2 oz. RedRum
½ oz. triple sec
3 oz. pineapple juice
1 oz. coconut syrup or milk
¼ oz. grenadine
pineapple slice for garnish

Pour into a tall glass. Garnish with pineapple slice.

RED HOT MAMA

1¼ oz. Bacardi Silver rum
4 oz. cranberry juice
2 oz. chilled club soda

RED RHUMBA

2 oz. RedRum
¼ oz. triple sec
3 oz. pineapple juice
1 oz. orange juice
¼ oz. grenadine
½ fresh banana
cherry for garnish

Blend with ice. Serve in a highball glass and garnish with cherry.

REDRUM ON THE BEACH

2 oz. RedRum
1 oz. 7UP
1½ oz. orange juice
½ oz. Grand Marnier

Mix with ice. Serve over ice.

REDRUM TSUNAMI

2 oz. RedRum
5 oz. pineapple juice
½ oz. melon liqueur
fresh fruit for garnish

Pour first two ingredients into a tall glass and mix with ice. Float the melon liqueur. Garnish with fresh fruit and an umbrella.

RED VELVET VICE

2 oz. 267 Infusion mango rum
½ oz. 267 cranberry vodka
splash orange vodka
orange wedge for garnish

Serve on the rocks with an orange wedge garnish.

REGGAE PUNCH

2 oz. Wray & Nephew rum
1 oz. orange juice
2 oz. pineapple juice
½ lime
2 heaping tbsp. brown sugar
¼ oz. grenadine or strawberry syrup

Mix first five ingredients over ice and pour into a highball glass. Top with grenadine or strawberry syrup.

RESERVE MAI TAI

1 oz. Whaler's Rare Reserve rum
1 oz. Whaler's Great White rum
1 oz. orgeat syrup
1 oz. passion fruit juice
3 oz. orange juice
½ oz. lime juice
maraschino cherries for garnish
orange slice for garnish

Shake well with ice and pour into a chilled hurricane glass. Garnish with maraschino cherries, orange slice, and an umbrella.

RICCO

1 oz. Bacardi Rum
½ oz. Grand Marnier
½ oz. grapefruit juice
½ oz. orange juice
2 oz. pineapple juice
pineapple slice for garnish
cherry for garnish

Shake and serve in a Collins glass. Garnish with pineapple slice and cherry.

RIKI TIKI

2 oz. Whaler's Pineapple Paradise rum
1 oz. triple sec
3 oz. sour mix
splash club soda

Shake the first three ingredients with ice and top with club soda.

ROOTS 'N' CULTURE

2 oz. Wray & Nephew rum
4 raspberries
3 strawberries
5 blueberries
½ lime
2 heaping tbsp. brown sugar

Muddle fruit and sugar. Build in a highball glass over crushed ice.

ROYAL DAIQUIRI

1½ oz. Appleton Estate V/X Jamaica rum
½ banana
juice of ¼ lime
1 tsp. sugar
1 scoop crushed ice
banana slice for garnish

Blend first five ingredients and serve in a cocktail glass. Garnish with banana slice.

ROYAL TEA

¼ oz. Captain Morgan Original spiced rum
1 oz. Crown Royal whiskey
¼ oz. peach schnapps
splash sour mix
4 oz. cola
lemon wedge for garnish

Shake first four ingredients with ice and pour into a glass. Top with cola. Garnish with lemon wedge.

RUBI REY MANHATTAN

1 oz. Ruby Rey rum
½ oz. Martini & Rossi red vermouth
maraschino cherry for garnish

Shake with cracked ice and strain into a cocktail glass. Garnish with maraschino cherry.

RUM HOT TODDY

⅔ cup Whaler's spiced rum
¼ cup sugar
2 tbsp. honey
3 cups boiling water
4 cinnamon sticks for garnish
4 lemon slices for garnish

Spread sugar on small plate. Dip rims of 4 mugs into cold water. Dip moistened rims of mugs into sugar. Mix rum and honey in 4-cup measuring cup. Add 3 cups boiling water; stir to blend. Divide Hot Toddy among prepared mugs. Garnish each mug with a cinnamon stick and a lemon slice.

RUM MILK PUNCH

1¾ oz. Rhum Barbancourt
¾ oz. sugar cane syrup
4 oz. milk
grated nutmeg for sprinkling

Blend first three ingredients and pour into a glass. Sprinkle with grated nutmeg.

RUM-RITA

1 oz. Whaler's Great White rum
1 oz. triple sec
1 oz. lime juice
salt to rim glass
lime wedge for garnish

Mix first three ingredients with ice and pour over ice into a salt-rimmed margarita glass. Garnish with lime wedge.

RUM RUNNER

¾ oz. Captain Morgan Original spiced rum
¼ oz. blackberry liqueur
¼ oz. crème de banana liqueur
2 oz. orange juice
½ oz. grenadine

Blend with 1 cup crushed ice until slushy and pour into a glass.

RUM RUSSIAN

2 oz. Brinley gold coffee rum
1 oz. vodka
3 oz. milk

Serve in a tall glass.

RUM SNATCH

2 oz. Alnwick rum
3 oz. orange juice
¼ oz. DeKuyper grenadine
¼ oz. lime juice

Pour the grenadine into a glass, then blend the Alnwick rum, orange juice, and lime juice together and pour carefully over the grenadine. Do not stir before serving.

RUMMY SOUR

1¼ oz. Captain Morgan Original spiced rum
1¾ oz. lemon-lime mix

Blend with a scoop of crushed ice.

RUSSIAN SEAL

1 oz. Gosling's Black Seal rum
1 oz. Kahlúa
fresh milk to top

Shake first two ingredients with ice and serve on the rocks. Top with fresh milk.

SANDBAR SMASH

1 oz. Cruzan citrus rum
1 oz. Cruzan pineapple rum
splash raspberry liqueur
2 oz. orange juice

Pour first three ingredients into a glass over ice and top with orange juice.

SAN JUAN COCKTAIL

1½ oz. Bacardi light rum
1 oz. grapefruit juice
½ oz. lemon or lime juice
¼–½ oz. Coco Lopez real cream of coconut
¼ oz. Bacardi 151 rum

Blend first four ingredients. Float Bacardi 151 rum.

SAN JUAN SIDECAR

1½ oz. Bacardi light rum
1 oz. lemon or lime juice
½ oz. white crème de menthe
sugar to rim glass
lime wheel for garnish

Serve in a sugar-rimmed glass and garnish with a lime wheel.

SAN JUAN SLING

1½ oz. Puerto Rican rum
¾ oz. cherry brandy
3 oz. sweetened lemon mix
½ oz. grenadine

Blend first three ingredients. Float grenadine.

SANTA'S SECRET SAUCE

1 oz. VooDoo spiced rum
1 oz. vodka
1 oz. Cointreau
5 oz. eggnog
grated nutmeg to top

Heat eggnog and combine with VooDoo spiced rum, vodka, and Cointreau in a mug. Top with nutmeg.

SCORPION

1 oz. light rum
½ oz. brandy
½ oz. gin
1 oz. sweet and sour mix
2 oz. orange juice
dash white crème de menthe
dash bitters
1 oz. white wine

Blend first seven ingredients. Float white wine. Garnish with an orchid.

SCREAM SODA

1¼ oz. Captain Morgan Original spiced rum
5 oz. lemon-lime soda
lemon slice for garnish
lime slice for garnish

Serve on the rocks. Garnish with lemon and lime slices.

SECRET PLACE

1½ oz. Puerto Rican dark rum
½ oz. cherry brandy
2 tsp. dark créme de cacao
4 oz. cold coffee

Stir with crushed ice.

SEX ON BARBADOS (PARTY RECIPE)

8 oz. Admiral Nelson's raspberry rum
8 oz. Arrow peach schnapps
8 oz. Arrow melon liqueur
8 oz. Arrow raspberry liqueur
1½ qt. pineapple juice
1½ qt. cranberry juice

Mix first four ingredients in a large pitcher or punch bowl. Add ice and fill with pineapple and cranberry juice. Makes 1 gallon of punch.

SEX ON THE BOAT

1 oz. Captain Morgan Original spiced rum
¼ oz. créme de banana
4½ oz. orange juice

Blend with a scoop of crushed ice.

SHILLELAGH

1 oz. Captain Morgan Original spiced rum
½ oz. green créme de menthe
2 oz. sweet and sour mix
green cherry for garnish

Pour into a pilsner glass over ice. Garnish with green cherry.

SHIPWRECK

1½ oz. Admiral Nelson's Premium spiced rum
2 oz. orange juice
2 oz. pineapple juice
splash cranberry juice
orange slice for garnish

Mix and serve over ice. Garnish with orange slice.

SHIP'S DOCTOR

2 oz. Admiral Nelson's Premium vanilla rum
1 oz. Arrow amaretto
8 oz. Dr. Pepper

Mix in a tall glass over ice.

SHIP'S MATE

1 oz. dark Jamaican rum
½ oz. white crème de cacao
½ oz. white crème de menthe
½ oz. sweet vermouth

Shake with ice. Serve in a chilled martini glass.

SHOOTING STARR

2 oz. Starr African rum
¾ oz. simple syrup
3 seedless black grapes
½ lemon
8 mint leaves

Muddle lemon, mint, and grapes in simple syrup. Add Starr African rum and cracked ice. Shake and pour into a rocks glass.

SHOWTUNE

1 oz. Captain Morgan Original spiced rum
¼ oz. amaretto
3 oz. grapefruit juice
1 tsp. grenadine
2 oz. club soda

Stir first four ingredients in a glass over ice. Add the soda and stir gently.

SIENNA

¾ oz. Captain Morgan Original spiced rum
½ oz. amaretto
2 oz. orange juice
1 oz. ginger ale

Pour into a tall wine glass over ice cubes.

SKIPPER TOO

1 part Malibu mango rum
½ part peach schnapps
½ part fresh lime
½ part Rose's lime
½ part sour mix
2 mint springs for garnish

Shake with ice and serve straight up or on the rocks. Garnish with mint sprigs.
    Developed by Happy Endings Bar, NYC.

SLAPSTICK

¾ oz. Captain Morgan Original spiced rum
½ oz. strawberry liqueur
1 oz. cream of coconut
1 oz. strawberry syrup or grenadine
2 oz. pineapple juice

Blend with 2 cups crushed ice until slushy.

SLIPPERY BANANA

½ part Malibu coconut rum
½ part Malibu Tropical banana rum
½ part splash pineapple juice
dash maraschino cherry juice (for color)

Developed by Happy Endings Bar, NYC.

SNOWBERRY

1¾ oz. Captain Morgan Original spiced rum
½ oz. strawberry schnapps
4 oz. water
½ oz. simple syrup
½ oz. lemon juice
1 tsp. grenadine
cinnamon stick for garnish

Heat and serve in a heated mug. Garnish with cinnamon stick.

SPANISH TOWN COCKTAIL

2 oz. Rhum Barbancourt
1 tsp. triple sec

Stir and strain into a glass with crushed ice.

SPICEBERRY

1¼ oz. Captain Morgan Original spiced rum
3 oz. strawberries
1 oz. cream of coconut

Blend with a scoop of crushed ice.

SPICED APPLE MARTINI

2½ oz. 10 Cane rum
2 oz. apple juice
splash amaretto
2 pinches ground cinnamon (plus more to rim glass)
superfine sugar to rim glass
cinnamon stick for garnish

Shake vigorously with ice and strain into a chilled cocktail glass rimmed with superfine sugar and ground cinnamon. Garnish with cinnamon stick.

SPICED BANANA DAIQUIRI

1 oz. Captain Morgan Original spiced rum
¼ oz. créme de banana
2 oz. sweet and sour mix
3 oz. banana (½ banana)
banana wheel for garnish
maraschino cherry for garnish

Blend thoroughly with 1 cup shaved ice. Pour into a 14-oz. glass. Garnish with banana wheel and maraschino cherry.

SPICED JAVA SMOOTH

1 oz. Captain Morgan Original spiced rum
½ oz. Godiva chocolate liqueur
½ oz. Godiva cappuccino liqueur
1 scoop ice cream
cherry for garnish

Blend until desired consistency. Pour into a glass and garnish with cherry.

SPICY ITALIAN

1 oz. VooDoo spiced rum
½ oz. Tuaca liqueur
5 oz. hot coffee
whipped cream to top

Pour first two ingredients into a mug. Fill with coffee and top with whipped cream.

SPUNKY GATOR

½ Stoli vodka
½ oz. gin
½ oz. rum
½ oz. Cuervo tequila
½ oz. triple sec
½ oz. melon liqueur
½ oz. blue curaçao
orange juice
lemon and orange wedges for garnish

Shake first seven ingredients and pour over ice. Top with orange juice.
Garnish with lemon and orange wedges.
*   From the Spunktown Tavern, Englesville, PA.*

STARR AFRICAN HONEY QUEEN

1½ oz. Starr African rum
½ oz. whipped cream
½ oz. honey syrup
¼ oz. amaretto

Shake well with ice and pour into a rocks glass.

STARR COBBLER

2 oz. Starr African rum
1 oz. curaçao
1 orange slice (plus another for garnish)
1 cherry (plus another for garnish
¼ lemon
½ lime
lemon wedge for garnish
lime wedge for garnish

Muddle fruit. Add Starr African rum and curacao. Shake and strain into a rocks glass over crushed ice. Garnish with an orange slice, a cherry, a lemon wedge, and a lime wedge.

STARR HONEYSUCKLE

2 oz. Starr African rum
¾ oz. lime juice
¾ oz. honey syrup

Shake violently and strain into a chilled cocktail glass.

STARR STRUCK

1½ oz. Starr African rum
1 oz. passion fruit puree
½ oz. strawberry puree
1 oz. simple syrup
¾ oz. grenadine
1 oz. champagne
½ strawberry for garnish

Shake first five ingredients in a Boston glass and strain into a champagne flute. Top with champagne. Garnish with ½ strawberry.

STING WRAY

1½ oz. Appleton Estate V/X Jamaica rum
5 oz. Ting or other grapefruit soda

Pour into a Collins glass over ice.

STONE & GRAVEL

2 oz. Wray & Nephew rum
2½ oz. Stones ginger wine

Pour into a Collins glass over crushed ice and stir.

STRAWBERRY TROPICOLADA

1¼ oz. Captain Morgan Parrot Bay rum
½ cup fresh hulled strawberries
4 oz. pineapple juice
2 oz. milk

Pour into a glass over ½ cup ice.

SUFFERING BASTARD

¼ oz. Sailor Jerry Spiced Navy rum
¼ oz. vodka
¼ oz. gin
¼ oz. blue curaçao
dash cherry brandy
3 oz. sour mix
3 oz. orange juice
orange wheel for garnish

Pour into a hurricane glass over ice and stir. Garnish with orange wheel.

SUMMER IN BELIZE

1½ oz. One Barrel rum
¾ oz. guava nectar
½ oz. orange juice
orange twist for garnish

Shake with ice and strain into a rocks glass over fresh ice. Garnish with orange twist.

SUMMERTIME

1 oz. Gosling's Black Seal rum
1 oz. Grand Marnier or Cointreau
2 tbsp. fresh lemon juice
lemon slice for garnish
lemon twist for garnish

Shake vigorously with ice and strain into a martini glass. Garnish with a lemon slice and a lemon rind twist.

SUNSPLASH

¾ oz. Captain Morgan spiced rum
¾ oz. Coco Lopez real cream of coconut
1¼ oz. Frangelico liqueur
5 oz. orange juice

Shake.

SUNTAN

1 oz. Kokocaribe coconut rum
1 oz. Baileys Irish cream

Layer in a shot glass.

SURFER ON X

Equal parts:
   coconut rum
   pineapple juice
   Agwa coco leaf liqueur

Serve on the rocks or shake as a shot.

SURF'S UP

1 oz. Gosling's Gold Bermuda rum
½ oz. Southern Comfort
½ oz. banana liqueur
1 oz. peach brandy
1 oz. fresh orange juice
dash grenadine
⅛ oz. toasted coconut for garnish

Blend first 6 ingredients with a cup of ice until smooth. Pour into large chilled goblets. Sprinkle with toasted coconut. A spoon may be necessary. If you have a flair for the dramatic, serve in halved coconut shells with all but a ⅛ inch of coconut meat removed.

SWEET SURRENDER

2½ oz. Baileys caramel
¼ oz. Captain Morgan rum
1 tbsp. ground macadamia nuts
1 tbsp. shaved Godiva white chocolate

From Jill Meyer—Graze, Orlando, FL.

TANGORU

1½ oz. Hiram Walker tangerine schnapps
1½ oz. Malibu Tropical banana rum

Shake with ice and pour into a chilled martini glass. Serve straight up or on the rocks.

TATTOO

1½ oz. Captain Morgan Tattoo rum

Serve chilled in a shot glass.

THE TEMPTATION

2 oz. Gosling's Gold Bermuda rum
¾ oz. orange liqueur or triple sec
2 oz. cranberry juice

Shake vigorously with ice and strain into a martini glass.

TENNESSEE TWISTER

1½ oz. Prichards' Fine Tennessee rum
½ oz. triple sec
splash sweet and sour mix
splash 7UP or Sprite
lime squeeze

Serve in a medium-high glass and garnish with a squeeze of lime.
  This tasty drink is featured at Cotton Eyed Joe's in Knoxville, TN.

THREE MILE ISLAND

2 oz. RedRum
4 oz. cranberry juice
½ oz. grapefruit juice
lime wedge for garnish

Mix first three ingredients in a tall glass with ice and garnish with lime wedge.

THUNDERBOLT

1 oz. Stroh Original 80 rum
1 oz. Aftershock liqueur
few drops Tabasco

Serve as a shot.

THE TIKI

1½ oz. Sailor Jerry Spiced Navy rum
2 oz. cranberry juice
2 oz. pineapple juice
splash sour mix
1 oz. orange curaçao
pineapple slice for garnish
orange slice for garnish
cherry for garnish

Shake first four ingredients with ice and pour into a Collins glass. Float orange curaçao on top. Garnish with pineapple slice, orange slice, and cherry.

TIKI SOUR

1½ oz. Seven Tiki rum
⅔ oz. lemon juice
½ oz. gomme or sugar syrup
cinnamon sugar to rim glass

Rim a chilled martini glass with cinnamon sugar. Shake sharply with ice and strain into cinnamon sugar-rimmed glass.

TOMMY'S BEE

1¾ oz. Tommy Bahama White Sand rum
½ oz. Barenjager honey liqueur
⅓ oz. orange juice
⅓ oz. fresh-squeezed lime juice
lime wedge for garnish

Shake sharply with ice and strain into a glass. Garnish with a wedge of lime.

TONY'S NOT-YET-FAMOUS RUM PUNCH

1 oz. Pyrat XO Reserve rum
1 oz. Velvet Falernum syrup
juice of 1 small lime
3 oz. fresh-squeezed orange juice
2 dashes Angostura bitters
pinch freshly grated nutmeg
pineapple spear for garnish
mint sprig for garnish

Shake with ice until well blended. Strain into a 16-oz. goblet over ice.
Garnish with spent lime shell, pineapple spear, and mint sprig.

TOP-SHELF LONG ISLAND

¼ oz. Captain Morgan Original spiced rum
¼ oz. Ciroc vodka
¼ oz. Don Julio Blanco tequila
¼ oz. Tanqueray London dry gin
¼ oz. Grand Marnier
splash sweet and sour mix
1 oz. cola

Shake with ice and pour into a tall glass.

TOP TEN

1¼ oz. Captain Morgan Original spiced rum
2 oz. cola
1 oz. cream of coconut
2 oz. heavy cream

Serve over a scoop of crushed ice.

TORTUGA BANANA BREEZE

2 oz. Tortuga banana rum
1 oz. lime juice
½ oz. banana liqueur or triple sec
1 banana, peeled and sliced

Blend with ½ cup crushed ice.

TORTUGA COLADA

2 oz. Tortuga coconut rum
4 oz. pineapple juice
1 oz. cream of coconut

Shake or blend with cracked ice.

TORTUGA PIRATE PUNCH

2 oz. Tortuga spiced rum
2 oz. mango nectar
2 oz. pineapple juice
½ oz. orange juice
½ oz. lime juice
splash grenadine

Shake with ice. Serve in a tall glass.

TREASURE

1¼ oz. Captain Morgan Original spiced rum
¼ oz. Goldschlager

Serve as a shot.

TRIP TO THE BEACH

½ oz. Malibu rum
½ oz. peach schnapps
½ oz. Smirnoff vodka
3 oz. orange juice

Serve over ice.

TROPIC FREEZE

1¼ oz. Captain Morgan Original spiced rum
2 oz. orange juice
2 oz. pineapple juice
1½ oz. cream of coconut
½ oz. grenadine
pineapple slice for garnish

*Blend with 12 oz. crushed ice until smooth. Serve in a specialty glass.
Garnish with pineapple slice.*

TROPICAL BANANA BALL

1 part Malibu Tropical banana rum
½ part melon liqueur

*Shake with ice and serve in a shot glass.
    Developed by Bamboo 52, NYC.*

TROPICAL BANANA DROP

1 oz. Malibu Tropical banana rum
1 oz. Stoli Citros vodka
¼ oz. lemon juice
⅛ oz. simple syrup

*   Developed by 40C, NYC.*

TROPICAL BREEZE

1¼ oz. Captain Morgan Original spiced rum
4 oz. cranberry juice
mint sprig for garnish

Serve on the rocks. Garnish with mint.

TROPICAL DELIGHT

½ oz. Captain Morgan Original spiced rum
¼ oz. crème de cacao
½ oz. crème de banana
3 oz. half-and-half
pinch nutmeg for garnish

Shake well and pour into a cocktail glass over ice. Garnish with nutmeg.

TROPICAL ITCH

1 oz. RedRum
1 oz. vodka
½ oz. Grand Marnier
3 oz. passion fruit juice

Shake with ice and pour into a tall glass.

TROPICAL PARADISE

1¼ oz. Captain Morgan Original spiced rum
2 oz. orange juice
½ banana
2 oz. cream of coconut
¼ oz. grenadine
pineapple slice for garnish

Blend with 1 cup crushed ice until smooth. Serve in a specialty glass. Garnish with pineapple slice and a palm tree stirrer.

TROPICAL TINI

2 oz. Whaler's Paradise pineapple rum
1 oz. Burnett's vanilla vodka
splash orange juice

Stir with ice and serve in a martini glass.

TROPICAL TREASURE

2½ oz. Captain Morgan Parrot Bay passion fruit rum
¼ oz. peach schnapps
2 oz. orange juice
splash grenadine
2 oz. cream

Pour into a highball glass over ice. Stir.

TROPICAL WAVE

1¼ oz. Captain Morgan Original spiced rum
4 oz. orange juice
1 oz. cranberry juice
pineapple slice for garnish

Shake with ice and pour into a tall glass. Garnish with pineapple slice.

TROPICO 2000 COCKTAIL

2 oz. Bacardi 151 rum
2 oz. Bacardi Tropico
drop Martini & Rossi sweet vermouth

Shake with ice. Serve over fresh ice in a tall glass.

TRUE PASSION

1½ oz. Tommy Bahama Golden Sun rum
½ oz. raspberry liqueur
1 oz. orange juice
2 oz. passion fruit juice
1 oz. sweet and sour
champagne to top

Pour first five ingredients into a chimney glass over ice. Top with champagne and garnish with a fresh orchid.

TWISTED ISLAND BREEZE

2½ oz. Captain Morgan Parrot Bay pineapple rum
2 oz. grapefruit juice
splash cranberry juice
2 oz. pineapple juice
pineapple slice for garnish

Pour into a highball glass over ice and stir. Garnish with pineapple slice.

UNDER THE COVERS

1 oz. Gosling's Black Seal rum
½ oz. bourbon
½ oz. Galliano
4–5 oz. hot chocolate
2 oz. heavy cream
grated chocolate for sprinkling

Pour first three ingredients into a heat-proof Irish coffee mug and stir. Add the hot cocoa. Float cream on top and sprinkle with grated chocolate.

VAMPIRE

2 oz. Cruzan vanilla rum
2 oz. lemon-lime soda
splash grenadine

Pour Cruzan vanilla rum into a highball glass over ice. Fill with lemon-lime soda and top with grenadine.

VANILLE CHERRY

1 oz. Whaler's Vanille rum
juice of 1 lime
½ oz. triple sec
½ oz. cherry-flavored brandy
orange wedge for garnish

Shake with ice and pour into a chilled cocktail glass. Garnish with orange wedge.

VANILLE PASSION

1 oz. Whaler's Vanille rum
1 oz. passion fruit juice
3 oz. orange juice
1 oz. Midori melon liqueur

Serve over ice.

VANILLE SPLASH

1½ oz. Whaler's Vanille rum
5 oz. pineapple juice
lime squeeze
cherries for garnish

Mix and pour into a margarita glass or a cocktail glass over ice. Garnish with cherries.

VANILLE SUNRISE

1 oz. Whaler's Vanille rum
4 oz. orange juice
1 oz. grenadine

Mix and pour into a Collins glass over ice.

VELVET ROSA

1⅔ oz. Tommy Bahama White Sand rum
⅓ oz. peach schnapps
1 oz. cranberry juice
champagne to top

Shake first three ingredients quickly with ice. Strain into a chilled glass and top with champagne. Stir quickly and garnish with a small flower.

VICIOUS SID

1½ oz. Puerto Rican light rum
½ oz. Southern Comfort
½ oz. Cointreau or triple sec
1 oz. lemon juice
dash bitters

Shake with ice. Serve over ice.

VIRGIN-ISLAND COFFEE

1 oz. VooDoo spiced rum
1 oz. Kahlúa
½ oz. cream
5 oz. hot coffee
whipped cream to top

Pour first three ingredients into a mug. Fill with coffee and top with whipped cream.

VOODOO DOLL

2 oz. VooDoo spiced rum
4 oz. Rockstar energy drink
lemon for garnish

Mix in a tall glass over ice. Garnish with lemon.

VOODOO MAGIC

2 oz. VooDoo spiced rum
Equal parts:
   7UP
   sweet and sour mix
splash cranberry juice
squeeze of lemon

Shake first three ingredients with ice. Add cranberry juice and a big squeeze of lemon. Serve as a shot.

VOODOO VOLCANO

1 oz. VooDoo spiced rum
1 oz. Kahlúa
½ oz. cream

Shake with ice. Strain into a shot glass and shoot it!

VOYAGER

1½ oz. Captain Morgan Original spiced rum
¼ oz. créme de banana
6 oz. hot apple cider

Pour the cider into a mug. Stir in the Captain Morgan Original spiced rum and crème de banana.

V/XTASY

2 oz. Appleton Estate V/X Jamaica rum
1½ oz. triple sec
½ oz. orange juice
1 oz. pineapple juice
¼ oz. grenadine
cherry or orange slice for garnish

Fill shaker halfway with ice. Add Appleton Estate V/X Jamaica rum, then grenadine, orange juice, and pineapple juice. Finally, add the triple sec and shake vigorously. Pour into a tall glass. Top with cherry or orange slice.

WALTZING BANANA

1 part Malibu Tropical banana rum
1 part blue curaçao
pineapple juice to fill

Serve over ice.
    Developed by 40C, NYC.

THE WAVE CUTTER

1½ oz. Mount Gay rum
1 oz. cranberry juice
1 oz. orange juice

Shake.

WELCOME 10

2 oz. 10 Cane rum
4 chunks fresh pineapple
fresh ginger to taste
splash fresh-squeezed lime juice
splash simple syrup
1 tsp. sugar in the raw
1 oz. pineapple juice

In a highball glass, muddle the pineapple, ginger, sugar in the raw, lime juice, and simple syrup. Add ice cubes, 10 Cane rum, and pineapple juice. Stir and garnish with a pineapple leaf.
    From Jeffrey Pogash, Director of Communications, Moët Hennessey USA.

WHALEBONE

1 oz. Tanduay 5 Years Rhum (or Tanduay Dark Rhum)
¼ oz. grenadine
½ oz. lemon juice
2 oz. soda water
juice of ½ lime or calamansi
pineapple slice for garnish
½ calamansi for garnish
red cherry for garnish

Stir with cracked ice and serve in an 8-oz. highball glass. Garnish with a slice of pineapple, a shell or half of a calamansi, and a red cherry.

WHALE'S BREATH

1 oz. Whaler's spiced rum
1 oz. cranberry juice
4 oz. orange juice
lime wedge for garnish

Mix with ice and pour into a glass over ice. Garnish with lime wedge.

THE WILD HURRICANE

1 oz. Wray & Nephew rum
1 oz. Appleton V/X rum
1 oz. Appleton white rum
¼ oz. orange curaçao
¼ oz. apricot brandy
¼ oz. fresh lime juice
3 oz. fresh orange juice
3 oz. pineapple juice
3 oz. grenadine syrup
⅛ oz. peeled banana
banana slice for garnish

Shake sharply with ice and strain into a glass with fresh ice. Garnish with banana slice.

WINTER IN TRINIDAD

1½ oz. 10 Cane rum
½ oz. Navan
2 oz. half-and-half
1 tbsp. powdered sugar
cinnamon for garnish

Combine 10 Cane, Navan, half-and-half, and powdered sugar in a mixing glass. Add ice and shake vigorously. Strain into a chilled martini glass. Garnish with ground cinnamon.

WITCH DOCTOR

1½ oz. VooDoo spiced rum
5 oz. Dr. Pepper
fresh lime for garnish

Pour VooDoo spiced rum into a glass over ice, top with Dr. Pepper, and stir. Garnish with a fresh lime.

X-TREME COLADA

2 oz. Appleton Estate V/X Jamaica rum
2 oz. pineapple juice
¾ oz. sweet cream
¾ oz. cream of coconut
pineapple wedge for garnish

Blend with 1 scoop crushed ice. Serve in a colada or rocks glass. Garnish with pineapple wedge.

YELLOW BIRD

1¾ oz. Bacardi rum
¼ oz. Liquore Galliano
¼ oz. Hiram Walker crème de banana
2 oz. pineapple juice
2 oz. orange juice

Shake with ice and serve in a tall glass.

ZIGGY'S STARRDUST

2 oz. Starr African rum
1 oz. pineapple juice
1 oz. orange juice
splash sweet and sour
splash grenadine
lemon juice to rim glass
sugar to rim glass

Coat the rim of a martini glass with lemon juice. Place sugar on a plate and dip the rim of the glass in the sugar. Shake first four ingredients with ice and strain into the sugar-rimmed martini glass. Slowly pour a splash of grenadine into the glass so that it sinks to the bottom, creating a multicolored layer.

ZOMBIE 151°

1 oz. Gosling's Gold Bermuda rum
1 oz. Gosling's Black Seal rum
1 oz. apricot brandy
½ oz. triple sec (or Cointreau)
½ oz. grenadine
2 oz. orange juice
2 oz. sour mix
⅛ oz. Rose's lime juice
½ oz. Gosling's Black Seal 151°
lemon slice for garnish
lime slice for garnish

Shake first eight ingredients in a large mixing glass 3/4 filled with cracked ice. Strain into a large Collins or highball glass. Top with Gosling's Black Seal 151°. Garnish with a slice each of lemon and lime.

ZOMBIE HUT'S COME-ON-I-WANNA-LEI-YA

2 parts Malibu Tropical banana rum
½ part Malibu passion fruit rum
splash pineapple juice

Shake and strain into shot glasses.
Developed by Zombie Hut, NYC.

ZOMBIE HUT'S MAMA'S GONE BANANAS

1 part Malibu Tropical banana rum
½ part Malibu coconut rum
club soda to fill
splash grenadine
cherry for garnish

Serve with ice and garnish with cherry.
Developed by Zombie Hut, NYC.

50 FOOD RECIPES USING RUM

AVOCADO SOUP

¼ cup Puerto Rican rum
1 large (or 2 medium) ripe avocados, peeled, seeded, and chopped
1 cup chicken stock or broth
1 cup heavy cream
¼ cup lemon juice
salt and white pepper to taste

Blend first five ingredients until smooth. Season with salt and pepper to taste. Serve cold. Serves 4.

BACARDI DOUBLE-CHOCOLATE RUM CAKE

1 cup Bacardi dark rum
1 pkg. (18½ oz.) chocolate cake mix
1 pkg. chocolate instant pudding and pie filling
¾ cup water
½ cup vegetable oil
4 eggs
12 oz. semisweet chocolate, chopped

1 cup raspberry preserves
2 tbsp. shortening
1 oz. vanilla baking bar

Preheat oven to 350°F. Combine cake mix, pudding, eggs, ½ cup of the Bacardi dark rum, water, and oil in large mixing bowl. Using an electric mixer, beat at low speed until moistened. Beat at medium speed 2 minutes. Stir in 1 cup of chocolate pieces. Pour batter into greased 12-cup bundt pan or 10-inch tube pan. Bake 50 to 60 minutes until cake tests done. Cool in pan 15 minutes. Remove from pan; cool on rack.

In a small saucepan, heat raspberry preserves and remaining ½ cup Bacardi dark rum. Strain through a sieve to remove seeds. Place cake on a serving plate. Prick surface of cake with a fork. Brush raspberry glaze evenly over cake, allowing cake to absorb glaze. Repeat until all glaze has been absorbed.

In a bowl, combine remaining 1 cup chocolate pieces and shortening. Microwave on high 1 minute or until melted. Stir until smooth. Or, heat mixture over hot (not boiling) water until chocolate melts and mixture is smooth. Spoon chocolate icing over cake. Let stand 10 minutes. In a small bowl, combine vanilla baking bar and 1 tsp. water. Microwave on high 30 seconds or until melted. Or, melt over hot (not boiling) water. Drizzle on top of chocolate icing.

BACARDI PEACH COBBLER

For peach cobbler:
½ cup Bacardi light rum
6 cups peeled and sliced peaches or 2 20-oz. packages frozen peaches, thawed
½ cup brown sugar
3 tbsp. cornstarch
1 tbsp. lemon juice
2 tsp. butter
1 cup chopped walnuts

For streusel topping (optional):
1 cup biscuit mix
½ cup rolled oats
½ cup brown sugar
4 tbsp. margarine
½ tsp. cinnamon

To make peach cobbler:
Preheat oven to 375°F. In a large bowl, combine peaches, Bacardi light rum, brown sugar, cornstarch, lemon juice, and walnuts. Place in an oven-proof casserole dish. Dot with margarine. Set aside.

To make streusel topping:
In a small bowl, combine all topping ingredients. Working quickly with your fingers, mix until it resembles coarse meal.

To assemble:
Sprinkle streusel topping over peaches and bake for 45 minutes. Serve warm. If desired, top with vanilla or rum raisin ice cream.

BACARDI STRAWBERRY MOUSSE

½ cup Bacardi light rum
1 10-oz. pkg. frozen strawberries, thawed
1 cup sugar
2 pkgs. unflavored gelatin
2½ cups whipping cream, divided
½ cup water

Soften gelatin in ½ cup water. Heat over low heat until gelatin is dissolved. Cool to room temperature. Puree strawberries in food processor or blender. Add sugar and mix well. Add cooled gelatin and stir well. Place mixture in refrigerator until it starts to set. Whip 1½ cups of whipping cream. Remove strawberry mixture from refrigerator; add Bacardi light rum and mix well. Fold in whipped cream. Pour

in a 2-quart soufflé dish or serving bowl. Refrigerate. When firm, deco-
rate with remaining cream, whipped (1 cup), and fresh sliced straw-
berries. Serves 4 to 6.

BANANAS FOSTER

¼ cup (½ stick) butter
1 cup brown sugar
½ tsp. cinnamon
¼ cup banana liqueur
4 bananas, cut in half lengthwise and then halved
¼ cup dark rum
4 scoops vanilla ice cream

Combine butter, sugar, and cinnamon in a flambé pan or skillet. Place
the pan over low heat either on an alcohol burner or on top of the stove
and cook, stirring, until the sugar dissolves. Stir in the banana liqueur,
then place the bananas in the pan. When the banana sections soften and
begin to brown, carefully add the rum. Continue to cook the sauce until
the rum is hot, then tip the pan slightly to ignite the rum. When the
flames subside, lift the bananas out of the pan and place four pieces
over each portion of ice cream. Generously spoon warm sauce over the
top of the ice cream and serve immediately.
  Thanks to Brennan's, New Orleans, LA.

BREADED PORK CHOPS WITH HERBS

¼ cup Puerto Rican light rum
8 thin pork chops
½ cup cream
2 eggs
salt and freshly ground pepper
1 tsp. sweet basil
1 tsp. marjoram

1 tsp. oregano
seasoned bread crumbs
olive oil

Clean and trim the pork chops of any excess fat. Mix cream, Puerto Rican light rum, eggs, salt, pepper, sweet basil, marjoram, and oregano together. Dip each piece of pork in the cream mixture and then dredge in the seasoned bread crumbs. Heat the oil in a skillet and brown the chops on both sides. Cover and simmer until well done. Serves 4.

BURRITOS

¼ cup Bacardi light rum
1½ lbs. ground meat
¼ cup onion, finely chopped
1 tsp. salt
¼ tsp. freshly ground pepper
½ tsp. garlic powder
1 tbsp. chili powder
Tomato sauce (see below)
12 7-inch flour tortillas
1½ cups refried beans
oil for frying

Cook ground meat in a skillet until well browned. Add onion and season well with salt, pepper, garlic powder, and chili powder. Mix in Bacardi light rum and tomato sauce and continue to cook until well heated. Spread some of the refried beans on each of the tortillas and place a large spoonful of the meat mixture to one side. Fold the ends of the tortilla so that they cover the meat mixture and then roll the tortillas, starting with the side with the meat mixture. Place the burritos flap-side down in a skillet with oil and fry for several minutes. Turn so that all sides are evenly cooked. Remove from the pan and drain on paper towels. Serve immediately.

For tomato sauce:
2 tbsp. olive oil
½ medium onion, finely chopped
1 clove garlic, minced
½ tsp. dried basil
1 28-oz. can whole tomatoes, including juice, shredded with fingers
salt and freshly ground pepper to taste

Heat olive oil in a large skillet over medium heat. Add chopped onion and stir to coat. Reduce heat to low and cook until translucent. Add minced garlic and cook for 30 seconds. Add tomatoes and basil; season with salt and pepper. Bring to a low simmer, reduce heat to low, and cook uncovered until thickened, about 15 minutes.

BUTTERED BEETS

½ cup Puerto Rican light rum
2 16-oz. cans whole baby beets with liquid
¼ cup brown sugar
¼ cup butter (½ stick)
¼ cup raisins

Preheat oven to 325°F. Place beets and liquid in an ovenproof casserole dish. Sprinkle with brown sugar and add butter and Bacardi light rum. Add raisins. Cover and bake for approximately 20 minutes. Serves 6 to 8.

CANDIED YAMS

1 cup Bacardi light rum
2 28-oz. cans yams, drained
½–¾ cups brown sugar
½ tsp. nutmeg
3 tbsp. butter

1 cup orange juice
1 11-oz. can mandarin oranges
2 cups miniature marshmallows

Preheat oven to 350°F. Place yams in a large ovenproof casserole serving dish. Sprinkle brown sugar and nutmeg over the yams. Place butter in three areas of the dish. Pour orange juice over all. Place mandarin oranges over the top of the yams. Add Bacardi light rum. Sprinkle miniature marshmallows evenly over and around the top of the dish. Bake for 20 to 30 minutes or until the yams are thoroughly heated and the marshmallows melted. Serves 6 to 8.

CHEDDAR CHEESE SAUCE

2 tbsp. Bacardi light rum
1 tbsp. butter
1 tbsp. flour
½ cup milk
1 cup grated cheddar cheese
salt and white pepper, to taste
¼ tsp. dry mustard

Melt the butter in a saucepan and slowly stir in the flour until a roux is formed. Mix the milk and Bacardi light rum together. Slowly pour the mixture into the roux, stirring constantly with a wire whisk. When all of the milk mixture has been used, begin to add the cheddar cheese, a little at a time. Continue to stir the mixture as the cheese is added to keep the sauce fluid and smooth. Season with salt, white pepper, and dry mustard. Continue to stir and cook the sauce until slightly thickened.

CHERRIED HAM

½ cup Bacardi light rum
4 slices precooked ham, ½ - to 1-inch thick
3 tbsp. butter
½ tsp. dry mustard
ground cloves to taste
1 16-oz. can pitted cherries, drained and liquid reserved
1 tbsp. cornstarch

Clean and trim the ham slices of any excess fat. Melt butter in a large skillet and add Bacardi light rum, dry mustard, and ground cloves. Add cherries and a little of the reserved liquid. Place ham slices in the sauce and cook until the meat is heated through. Mix cornstarch with some of the reserved liquid and slowly add the mixture to the sauce until it begins to thicken. Adjust the seasoning to taste. Serve sauce and cherries warm over the ham slices. Serves 4.

CHICKEN CUT-UPS

¼ cup Puerto Rican light rum
¼ cup melted butter
¼ cup orange juice
½ tsp. grated orange rind
½ tsp. salt
⅛ tsp. ground ginger
⅛ tsp. pepper
1 garlic clove, crushed
1 lb. cut-up fryer chicken

Preheat oven to 350°F. Combine all liquids and seasonings. Brush chicken parts generously with the mixture. Arrange the chicken pieces skin-side up in a shallow baking pan, basting occasionally with the remaining mixture. Bake 1 hour or until golden and tender. Serves 4.

CHICKEN SALAD

⅛ cup Bacardi light rum
1 cup mayonnaise
⅛ cup sweet relish
⅛ cup catsup
2 cups cooked chicken
1 cup diced celery
½ head lettuce or avocado shells
dash paprika
8 pimento pieces

Mix first four ingredients in a bowl. Add the chicken and celery. Chill in the refrigerator before serving. Serve on a bed of lettuce or in avocado shells. Garnish with a sprinkle of paprika and pieces of pimento. Serves 4.

CHICKEN STICKS

3 tbsp. Bacardi dark rum
12 chicken wings
⅔ cup seasoned bread crumbs
1 oz. butter or margarine
salt and pepper, to taste

Cut chicken wings in half with a sharp knife. Place them in a shallow pan. Drizzle Bacardi dark rum over wings. Cover and chill for several hours, turning wings once or twice. Roll wings in the seasoned bread crumbs, coating well. Sauté in butter or margarine for 18 to 20 minutes. Sprinkle with salt and pepper. Makes 24 pieces.

COCONUT RICE & DRUNKEN PEAS

¼ cup Mount Gay Eclipse rum
1 cup dried red kidney beans (6 ½ oz.)
4 cups water
2 cans coconut milk
2 cups boiling water
5 tsp. kosher salt
2 scallions, trimmed and left whole
2 fresh thyme sprigs
1 whole green Scotch bonnet pepper or habanero chile
5 cups water
4 cups long-grain rice (not converted)

Simmer kidney beans in 4 cups water in a 5-quart saucepan, covered, until beans are almost tender, about 1¼ hours (do not drain). When almost tender, add Mount Gay Eclipse rum and let soak. Stir 1 can coconut milk into almost tender beans along with salt, scallions, thyme, and Scotch bonnet pepper or habanero chile, then simmer, covered, for 15 minutes.

Add 4½ cups water and bring to a boil. Stir in rice and return to a boil, then stir in second can of coconut milk. Cover. Reduce heat to low and cook until water is absorbed and rice is tender, about 20 minutes. Remove from heat and let stand, covered, for 10 minutes, then fluff with a fork. Discard scallions, thyme, and chile. Makes 10 to 12 side-dish servings.

CREAM OF MUSHROOM SOUP

¼ cup Bacardi light rum
½ lb. chopped mushrooms
¼ cup chopped onion
¼ cup chopped celery
5 cups chicken stock or broth
4 tbsp. butter

¼ cup flour
1 cup cream
salt and freshly ground pepper to taste

Place mushrooms, onion, and celery in a saucepan with chicken stock or broth and simmer for 20 minutes. Remove from heat and allow to cool slightly, then blend the ingredients into a puree. Return the soup to heat. Knead butter and flour together and whisk into the soup to thicken it. Add cream and season with salt and pepper to taste. Add Bacardi light rum and stir thoroughly, allowing the soup to simmer until heated through. Serves 4 to 6.

DAIQUIRI PIE

⅓ cup Puerto Rican light rum
1 pkg. (4-serving size) Jell-O brand lemon instant pudding and pie
   filling
1 3-oz. pkg. Jello-O lime-flavored gelatin
⅓ cup sugar
2½ cups water
2 eggs, slightly beaten
2 cups Cool Whip non-dairy whipped topping, thawed
1 baked 9-inch crumb crust, cooled

Mix pudding, gelatin, and sugar in a saucepan. Stir in ½ cup water and eggs; blend well. Add remaining water. Stir over medium heat until mixture comes to a full boil. Remove from heat; stir in Puerto Rican light rum. Chill about 1½ hours. (To hasten chilling, place bowl of filling mixture in larger bowl of ice and water; stir until mixture is cold.) Blend topping into chilled mixture. Spoon into crust. Chill until firm, about 2 hours. Garnish with additional whipped topping and lime or lemon slices, grated lime or lemon peel, or graham cracker crumbs.

FETTUCCINE A LA RUM

1 lb. fettuccine
salted boiling water
½ cup softened butter (1 stick)
1 cup heavy cream
½ cup Bacardi dark rum
2 cups grated Parmesan cheese
freshly ground black pepper, to taste
½ tsp. nutmeg

Cook fettuccine in salted boiling water until tender, approximately 4 to 5 minutes. Just before the fettuccine is done, melt butter in a casserole serving dish over low heat. Add some of the heavy cream, Bacardi dark rum, and parmesan cheese and stir thoroughly until smooth. When the fettuccine is ready, place the noodles in the casserole dish and toss gently to coat with the butter and cream mixture. Add remaining cream, Bacardi dark rum, and cheese, a little at a time, and continue to toss and mix the noodles. Season to taste with pepper and nutmeg. Serves 4 to 6.

FRESH CRANBERRY SAUCE

½ cup Bacardi light rum
4 cups fresh cranberries
½ cup orange juice
¾ cup sugar
¼ tsp. ginger
½ tsp. cloves
½ tsp. cinnamon

Clean and wash cranberries. Mix cranberries with orange juice and Bacardi light rum and bring to a boil in a saucepan. Continue to stir over medium heat and add the sugar and seasonings. Stir until dissolved. Cool until ready to serve, or serve warm. Makes approximately 4 cups.

FRUIT SALAD WITH PIÑA COLADA DRESSING

For dressing:
¼ cup Bacardi light rum
1 cup heavy cream
¼ cup banana yogurt
¼ cup pineapple juice
1 tbsp. coconut cream

For fruit salad:
5 lettuce leaves
½ cup desired fruits, peeled and sliced
½ cup shredded coconut

To make dressing:
In a medium bowl, whip cream until thickened but not stiff. Fold in yogurt, pineapple juice, Bacardi light rum, and coconut cream. Makes approximately 1¾ cups.

To assemble salad:
Arrange lettuce leaves on a large platter. Decoratively place fruit over lettuce. Sprinkle with coconut. Serve with dressing.

GUACAMOLE

2 ripe avocados, peeled, seeded, and mashed
1 tomato, peeled, seeded, and chopped
½ cup finely chopped scallions or onions
1 tbsp. lemon juice
salt to taste
freshly ground black pepper to taste
½ tsp. coriander
1 oz. Puerto Rican rum
½ tsp. chili powder
½ tsp. garlic powder

Mix ingredients thoroughly and chill before serving. Makes approximately 1½ cups.

HOLLANDAISE SAUCE

1½ tbsp. Puerto Rican rum
3 egg yolks
1½ tbsp. lemon juice
1½ tbsp. water
¼ lb. butter, melted
¼ tsp. salt

In the top of a double-boiler over (not in) hot water, beat the egg yolks until they begin to thicken. Mix the lemon juice, Puerto Rican rum, and water together and warm the mixture in a small saucepan. Slowly add the lemon mixture to the egg yolks while continuing to beat with a whisk. Slowly pour in the melted butter, a little at a time, while continuing to beat the sauce. Add the salt while you pour in the butter. Serve warm. Makes 1 cup.

MALIBU RUM CAKE

For cake:
1½ cups Malibu rum
1 pkg. yellow cake mix (no pudding)
1 pkg. instant vanilla pudding
4 eggs
1½ cups vegetable oil

For glaze:
½ cup Malibu rum
¼ lb. butter
¼ lb. water
1 cup sugar

To make cake:
Preheat oven to 325°F. Hand mix all ingredients. Bake in 12-cup bundt pan for one hour.

To make glaze:
Melt butter; stir in water and sugar. Boil 5 minutes, stirring constantly. Remove from heat and add Malibu rum. Let cool slightly before glazing cake.

MANGO FLAMBÉ

⅓ cup Mount Gay XO dark rum
4 1-lb. firm-ripe mangoes
½ cup raw brown sugar

Preheat oven to 400°F. Wash and dry mangoes. Remove 2 flat sides of each mango with a sharp knife, cutting lengthwise alongside the pit and cutting as close to the pit as possible so that mango flesh is in 2 large pieces. Make a crosshatch pattern with a small sharp knife. Grasp fruit at both ends and turn inside out to make flesh side convex.

Arrange fruit, skin-side down, in a large shallow baking pan lined with foil and sprinkle evenly with 4 tablespoons sugar. Bake in oven for 5–8 minutes until fruit is golden brown. (It will not brown evenly.) Arrange fruit on a large platter.

Cook Mount Gay XO dark rum with remaining sugar and butter in a small saucepan over moderately low heat, stirring, until sugar is dissolved. Remove from heat, then carefully ignite rum with a kitchen match and pour, still flaming, over warm mangoes. Serve immediately.

MARINATED CHICKEN

½ cup Puerto Rican dark rum
2 cups fresh orange juice
zest of 2 oranges
2 tbsp. chopped mint
⅛ oz. curry powder
½ oz. chopped cilantro
½ oz. minced garlic
¼ cup soy sauce
1 whole chicken, cut up

Combine all ingredients except chicken in a shallow baking dish. Place chicken in marinade overnight. Grill chicken, basting with marinade until done.

MINI-BALLS

1½ tbsp. Bacardi light rum
2 tbsp. soy sauce
1 garlic clove, pressed
1 tsp. ground ginger
1 lb. ground chuck

Preheat oven to 300°F. Blend the first four ingredients. Add the ground chuck and blend well. Shape into balls about 1-inch in diameter. Bake for 12 to 15 minutes, turning once. Serve with toothpicks.

MOCHA PIE

½ cup Puerto Rican dark rum
2 cups stiffly whipped cream
¼ cup sugar
1 graham cracker pie crust

½ oz. chunk sweet chocolate
⅛ tsp. cinnamon
⅛ oz. instant espresso granules

Combine whipped cream with sugar and Puerto Rican dark rum. Pour the mixture into crust. Grate chocolate on top. Sprinkle cinnamon and espresso over top, to taste.

MORGAN'S SPICY PEARS WITH VANILLA RUM CREAM

For vanilla rum cream:
¼ cup Captain Morgan spiced rum
1 pint vanilla ice cream, slightly softened

For pears:
⅓ cup Captain Morgan spiced rum
8 firm ripe pears
juice and grated peel of 1 lemon
½ cup apricot preserves
¼ cup vanilla cookie crumbs
¼ cup chopped almonds

To make vanilla rum cream:
Mix ice cream and Captain Morgan spiced rum. Freeze. Re-soften before serving.

To make pears:
Preheat oven to 350°F. Peel pears, leaving stems attached; core from bottom. Pour lemon juice over pears. In a saucepan, heat preserves, Captain Morgan spiced rum, and lemon peel until boiling. Coat pears with sauce, then roll in crumbs and nuts. Stand upright in baking dish with excess sauce; cook pears until tender, about 30 minutes.

Serve with rum cream. Serves 8.

ONION SOUP

½ cup Bacardi light or dark rum
2 onions, peeled and thinly sliced
butter for sauteing
6 cups beef broth
salt to taste
freshly ground pepper to taste
6 slices French bread, lightly toasted
grated Parmesan cheese
Gruyere cheese (optional)

Preheat oven to 275°F. Lightly sauté the sliced onions in butter until slightly browned. Add the beef broth and ¼ cup Bacardi light or dark rum and season to taste with salt and pepper. Cover and simmer over low heat for 30 minutes. Stir in ¼ cup Bacardi light or dark rum. Pour the soup into a casserole or 6 individual serving dishes. Place French bread (toasted slightly) over the soup and sprinkle Parmesan cheese on top. Place the dish or dishes in preheated oven for approximately 5 minutes, or until cheese has melted. Serve immediately. Serves 6.

PARMESAN CHEESE SPREAD

¼ cup Bacardi light rum
½ cup sour cream
1 cup grated Parmesan cheese
3 slices bacon, cooked and chopped

Mix the ingredients together thoroughly. Makes approximately 1½ cups.

To serve:
Spread the mixture on small slices of toast, cocktail rye bread, or small pieces of English muffin and run under the broiler for several minutes until golden.

PORK CHOPS WITH PINEAPPLE SAUCE

1 cup Bacardi light or dark rum
8 large, thick pork chops
salt and freshly ground pepper to taste
½ cup butter (1 stick)
2 cups crushed pineapple
1 cup golden raisins
4 tbsp. brown sugar
1 tbsp. cornstarch

Preheat oven to 350°F. Season pork chops with salt and pepper. Melt the butter in a saucepan and stir in Bacardi light or dark rum. Add crushed pineapple and raisins and continue to cook over low heat. Slowly stir in brown sugar and cornstarch, and continue to cook the sauce until it begins to thicken slightly. Place the pork chops in an ovenproof casserole dish and pour the sauce over the meat. Cover and bake for approximately 1 hour or until the pork is thoroughly cooked. Or, barbecue the pork chops to preferred doneness and use the pineapple sauce to baste the meat as it cooks. Turn once. Serve with extra sauce on the side. Serves 4 to 8.

ROAST TURKEY WITH STUFFING

¼ cup Bacardi light rum
1 10–12 lb. ready-to-cook turkey
1 tsp. rosemary
1 tsp. sage
1 tsp. thyme
1 tsp. basil
freshly ground pepper to taste
butter
Turkey Stuffing (see p. 280)

Preheat oven to 350°F. Clean the turkey and remove the innards. Mix seasonings together with Bacardi light rum and rub the inside of the turkey with the mixture. Stuff the turkey with prepared stuffing but do not pack too tightly; the stuffing will expand as it cooks. Truss the bird. Rub the outside of the turkey with butter and place it breast side up on a rack in a roasting pan. Place in the oven for 30 minutes. Reduce the heat to 325°F and cook for 20 to 25 minutes per pound. If parts of the turkey look like they may brown or burn too much, use foil to cover those areas. To test for doneness, pull the leg from the side. If it separates easily the turkey is ready. Serves 8.

RUM BALLS

¼ cup Bacardi dark rum
1½ cup vanilla wafer crumbs (about 50 cookies)
¼ cup honey
2 cups (8 oz.) ground walnuts
½ oz. confectioner's sugar

Blend first four ingredients thoroughly. Shape into small balls about 1 inch in diameter. Roll in sugar. Store in a tightly covered container. Makes about 2½ dozen.

RUM CUSTARD

1 oz. Bacardi Gold Reserve rum
2 cups half-and-half or cream
¼ cup sugar
⅛ tsp. salt
1 tbsp. cornstarch
4 egg yolks, lightly beaten
1 tsp. vanilla

Scald half-and-half or cream in the top of a double-boiler over (but not touching) boiling water. Add sugar, salt, and cornstarch, a little at a time, and stir until smooth. Stir in Bacardi Gold Reserve rum. Add egg yolks and slowly stir the mixture until it begins to thicken. Add vanilla and continue to stir slowly until the custard is thick. Remove from heat and allow to cool. Chill thoroughly before using. Makes approximately 2 cups.

SAUCE VINAIGRETTE

2 tbsp. Puerto Rican light rum
2–3 cloves garlic, finely minced
½ tsp. freshly ground pepper
1 tsp. salt
1½ cups walnut or olive oil
½ cup cider or wine vinegar
½ tsp. dry mustard (optional)
1 tsp. lemon juice (optional)
1 tbsp. mixed herbs (chervil, parsley, chives, etc.), optional

Mix the garlic, salt, and pepper in the bottom of a jar or glass container that has a lid. Add oil and vinegar, Puerto Rican light rum, and other ingredients, if desired. Close the lid tightly and shake vigorously. Chill in the refrigerator until ready to use. Shake vigorously before using.

SAUTÉED SCALLOPS

1 cup Bacardi light rum
1 lb. scallops
¼ cup butter (½ stick)
4 shallots, finely chopped
½ cup chopped mushrooms
1 tbsp. chopped fresh parsley
2 tbsp. flour

Place the scallops in a bowl and cover with the Bacardi light rum. Melt the butter in a skillet and sauté the shallots, mushrooms, and parsley *until tender. Slowly stir in the flour until well mixed and smooth. Add the scallops and Bacardi Light rum and stir until the sauce is thickened. Adjust seasoning to taste. Serves 3 to 4.*

SAUTÉED SHRIMP

1½ lb. medium shrimp, shelled and deveined
½ cup Puerto Rican light rum
¼ cup butter or margarine
½ tsp. garlic salt
⅓ cup grated Parmesan cheese
freshly ground pepper to taste

Marinate the shrimp in the Puerto Rican light rum for several hours. Melt butter or margarine in a large frying pan. Add shrimp and rum mixture with garlic salt. Sauté 8 to 10 minutes or until shrimp is cooked through. Sprinkle grated Parmesan cheese and ground pepper over shrimp. Broil for 2 to 3 minutes until cheese browns. Serve hot. Serves about 6.

SEASONED RICE

1 cup Puerto Rican rum
1 cup long-grain rice
½ cup chopped onion
butter
½ cup peeled, seeded, and chopped tomatoes
½ cup chopped celery
½ cup chopped mushrooms
1 tsp. salt
¼ tsp. freshly ground pepper
1 tsp. saffron
1 cup orange juice

Cook long-grain rice in lightly salted boiling water for approximately 10 minutes or until the rice is light and fluffy. While the rice is cooking, sauté chopped onion in butter until tender and golden. Add tomatoes, celery, and mushrooms and season with salt and pepper. When the rice is ready, mix saffron with Puerto Rican light rum and stir. Pour the mixture into the rice and mix until rum and saffron are thoroughly absorbed. Add the rice mixture to the vegetables and continue to stir and cook until thoroughly mixed. Add orange juice and continue to stir until most of the moisture is absorbed. Serve with any of your favorite seafood dishes.

SHRIMP IN ORANGE SAUCE

½ cup Bacardi light or dark rum
3 tbsp. butter
1 cup orange juice
½ cup honey
1–2 tsp. ginger
¼ tsp. cloves
1 lb. large shrimp, cooked, shelled and deveined

Melt butter in the top of a double-boiler over (not in) boiling water. Slowly stir in orange juice, Bacardi light or dark rum, and honey. Season the sauce with ginger and cloves. Continue to stir and cook for several minutes. Add the shrimp to the sauce and continue to cook until heated through. Serves 4 to 6.

SHRIMP JAMBALAYA

½ cup Bacardi light rum
1 onion, chopped
2 cloves garlic, finely chopped
butter
1 green pepper, seeded and chopped
¼ lb. mushrooms, chopped

2 tomatoes, peeled, seeded, and chopped
salt and freshly ground pepper to taste
½ cup chicken broth
1 lb. shrimp, shelled and deveined
3–4 cups long-grain rice, cooked

Sauté chopped onion and garlic in butter until golden and tender. Add chopped green pepper and continue to sauté the mixture. Add mushrooms and tomatoes and season with salt and pepper. Add more butter if needed. Pour in chicken broth and Bacardi light rum and continue to simmer over low heat. Add shrimp and cook for at least 5 minutes until the shrimp are done and heated through. Serve with cooked long-grain rice. Serves 4.

SHRIMP UNDER FIRE

2 tbsp. Bacardi dark rum
2 lbs. large, unshelled shrimp
½ cup Bacardi dark rum
½ stick butter, melted
¼ cup minced parsley
1 tbsp. lemon juice
2 crushed garlic cloves
1 tsp. salt
⅛ tsp. freshly ground pepper

Leaving the tails on, peel, devein, and rinse the shrimp. Cutting not quite through, split the shrimp lengthwise. Flatten slightly. Combine all remaining ingredients except the Bacardi dark rum in a shallow sauté or frying pan. Heat. Add shrimp, turning to coat well. Cook over low heat until shrimp turn pink and tender. Splash 2 tablespoons Bacardi dark rum over shrimp. Ignite shrimp immediately at table. Serves 6.

SOLE WITH LEMON CREAM SAUCE

½ cup Puerto Rican light rum
butter to grease baking dish
1½ lbs. fillet of sole
½ cup heavy cream
4 tbsp. lemon juice
1 tbsp. grated lemon rind
salt and freshly ground pepper to taste
1 tbsp. butter
1 tbsp. flour
lemon wedges
fresh parsley sprigs

Preheat oven to 400°F. Butter a large baking dish and arrange sole in a single layer. Mix heavy cream, Puerto Rican light rum, lemon juice, and rind together and pour over the fish. Season with salt and pepper. Bake, uncovered, for 20 minutes, or until the fish is done to preference. Remove fish from the baking dish and keep warm. Melt 1 tablespoon of butter over low heat and slowly stir in flour to make a roux. Slowly pour in the liquid from the baking dish, a little at a time, and continue to stir with a whisk until the sauce begins to thicken. Season to taste and serve the sauce warm over the fillet of sole. Garnish each serving with lemon wedges and fresh sprigs of parsley. Serves 2 to 3.

STEAK BAKE

½ cup Puerto Rican light rum
2 extra-large rib-eye steaks (at least ¾ lb. each), or your favorite cut
salt and freshly ground pepper to taste
1 tsp. garlic powder
1 cup catsup
2 tbsp. Worcestershire sauce
3 tbsp. lemon juice
½ cup chili sauce

Preheat oven to 400°F. Season steaks with salt, pepper, and garlic powder on both sides. Mix catsup, Puerto Rican light rum, Worcestershire sauce, lemon juice, and chili sauce together. Season to taste with salt, pepper, and garlic powder. Pour the sauce over the steaks in a shallow ovenproof casserole dish and allow the steaks to marinate in the sauce for at least 15 minutes. Bake the steaks for approximately 30 minutes or until done to preference, depending on the size and thickness. Baste the steaks as they cook; turn once. Serves 2.

STEAK BITES

1 cup Puerto Rican light or dark rum
1½ lbs. steak (your choice)
salt and freshly ground pepper
½ cup teriyaki sauce
1 tbsp. Worcestershire sauce
2–3 cloves garlic, finely chopped
½ tsp. dry mustard
½ oz. oil or butter

Cut steak into ?-inch pieces and trim any excess fat. Place the pieces in a bowl and season with salt and pepper. Add Puerto Rican light or dark rum, teriyaki sauce, Worcestershire sauce, garlic, and dry mustard. Marinate in the refrigerator for at least 1 hour. Remove the steak pieces and pan fry in oil or butter until well browned on all sides. Serve with toothpicks while hot. Makes approximately 20–30 appetizers.

STUFFED CHICKEN BREASTS

½ cup Puerto Rican light rum
8 boneless chicken breasts
salt and freshly ground pepper to taste
¾ oz. butter
6 shallots, finely chopped

8 tbsp. deviled ham
3 oz. Monterey Jack cheese

Pound chicken breasts until thin. Season with salt and pepper. Melt butter in a pan and sauté shallots until tender. Add the chicken breasts and cook for several minutes on each side. Add Puerto Rican light rum and continue to cook for several minutes more. Remove the chicken breasts from the pan and spread 1 tablespoon deviled ham (or more, to taste) on each breast. Cover the deviled ham with a slice of Monterey Jack cheese. Close the chicken over the stuffing and fasten with a toothpick. Return the stuffed chicken to the pan and continue to cook until the chicken is done and the cheese melts. Serves 4.

TERIYAKI MARINADE

½ cup Bacardi light rum
½ cup vegetable oil
½ cup soy sauce
4 tbsp. brown sugar
3 cloves garlic, finely minced
1 tbsp. fresh ginger root, chopped
1 tsp. rosemary (optional)
1 tsp. thyme (optional)

Mix ingredients in a bowl and stir thoroughly. Cover and keep in the refrigerator until ready to use. Use the marinade for steaks or poultry. Makes approximately 2 cups.

TROPICAL RUM PUNCH CHICKEN

1½ cups Rum Punch (½ cup orange juice, ½ cup pineapple juice, ½ cup rum)
¼ cup Mount Gay rum
1 3½–4 lb. chicken, cut into 8 serving pieces

1¾ tsp. salt
1½ tsp. black pepper
3 tbsp. unsalted pepper
1 cup chopped onion
1 tbsp. chopped garlic
1 large white onion, finely chopped
2 tsp. dried oregano, crumbled
1½ lb. russet (baking) potatoes
4 cups chicken broth
½ cup coconut cream
3 ears corn, cut crosswise into 1-inch pieces

Pat chicken dry and season with ¾ tsp. salt and ½ tsp. pepper. Heat butter in a wide, heavy, 7- to 8-quart pot over moderately high heat until foam subsides. Brown chicken in 2 batches, skin side down first, turning occasionally, for about 10 minutes. Transfer chicken as browned to a plate.

Add onion to the pot along with oregano and remaining salt and pepper, and sauté, stirring until light golden, about 5 minutes. Peel and coarsely grate russet potatoes. Add to the pot with chicken, broth, coconut cream, and ½ cup water. Simmer, covered, stirring occasionally until the chicken is cooked through, about 25 minutes. Add corn and simmer 10 minutes, covered.

TUNA CASSEROLE

¼ cup Puerto Rican rum
2 ½ cups cooked noodles
7 oz. tuna fish
½ tbsp. butter
10 oz. cream of mushroom soup
½ cup grated cheese
½ cup bread crumbs
½ cup Worcestershire sauce

Preheat oven to 425°F. Butter the bottom of an ovenproof casserole dish and cover with a layer of cooked noodles. Arrange flakes of the tuna fish over noodles and then cover with another layer of noodles. Continue creating layers until all of the noodles and tuna fish are used. Pour Puerto Rican rum over the noodle mixture. Add cream of mushroom soup and sprinkle with grated cheese and bread crumbs. Season with several dashes Worcestershire sauce. Cover and bake for 10 to 20 minutes until the cheese is melted thoroughly. Serves 4 to 6.

TURKEY STUFFING

1 cup Bacardi light rum
1 small onion
¼ lb. mushrooms, chopped
butter
½ cup raisins
1 cup chopped celery
½ cup chopped pecans
½ cup chopped walnuts
½ lb. sausage, cooked and chopped
1 cup apples, cooked and chopped
1 cup pineapple, crushed
8 cups soft bread crumbs
1 cup chicken stock or broth

Sauté onions and mushrooms in butter and set aside. Soak raisins in warm water for 5 to 10 minutes. Mix celery, pecans, walnuts, sausage, apples, pineapple, and raisins together in a large bowl. Add soft bread crumbs and toss the mixture until everything is thoroughly blended. Add chicken stock or broth and Bacardi light rum and continue to toss the mixture. Use the stuffing to fill a turkey. Any extra stuffing can be placed in a buttered dish, covered, and baked alongside the turkey. Do not stuff the turkey too tightly because the stuffing will expand when it cooks. Makes enough stuffing for a 12-pound turkey.

VEAL SCALLOPPINE

½ cup Puerto Rican light rum
1½ lbs. veal cutlet, trimmed of excess fat, pounded thin, and cut into
     1-to 2-inch pieces
flour, salt, and freshly ground pepper, as needed
garlic powder to taste (optional)
2–3 tbsp. butter
1 medium tomato, peeled, seeded, and chopped
½ lb. mushrooms, sliced
1 tsp. basil
1 tsp. oregano
2 tbsp. fresh parsley, chopped

Dredge veal pieces in flour and season with salt, pepper, and garlic powder. Melt butter in a skillet and sauté the veal until browned. Add Puerto Rican light rum, tomato, and mushrooms, and season with basil, oregano, and parsley. Continue to stir the sauce until it becomes smooth. Adjust seasoning to taste. Serves 2.

75 RUM PRODUCERS

Alberta Distillers Limited, Canada
Allied Domecq, United States
Alzola Distillery, Cardenas, Cuba
Angostura Ltd., Trinidad and Tobago
Anguilla Rums Ltd./Rum Pyrat, Anguila
Antigua Distillery Ltd., Antigua and Barbuda
Appleton Rum, Jamaica
Bacardi Global Brand Marketing, Bahamas
Barbancourt, Haiti
Barcelo & Co., Dominican Republic
Barton Brands, United States
Brinley & Co., United States
Brown-Forman, United States
Brugal, United States
Bundaberg, Australia
Captain Morgan, United States
Castle Brands, United States
Celebration Distillation, United States
Centenario Internacional, Costa Rica
Charbay Winery and Distillery, United States
Clement, Martinique
Conch Republic Rum Co., United States

Cruzan Rum Distillery, St. Croix
Cuba Ron SA, Cuba
David Sherman Corp. (Admiral Nelson), United States
Demerara's El Dorado Rum, United States
Destileria Serralles (Don Q Limon), Puerto Rico
Distillerie Bielle, Guadeloupe
Distillerie Bologne, Guadeloupe
Distillerie Damoiseau, Guadeloupe
Distillerie Depaz, Martinique
Distillerie Dillon, Martinique
Distillerie Neisson, Martinique
Domaine de Severin, Guadeloupe
Dominica Essential Oils and Spices Co-operative, Dominica
Don Lorenzo Rum of the Bahamas, Bahamas
DonQ-Me.com, Puerto Rico
Duquesne, Martinique
Ed Phillips & Sons, United States
Foursquare Distillery, Barbados
FRANK-LIN Distillers Products, Ltd., United States
Gosling Brothers, Bermuda
Grand Cayman Bottlers & Blenders, Cayman Islands
Havana Club Cuban Rum, Cuba
Heaven Hill Distilleries, United States
Highwood Distillers Ltd., Canada
Hood River Distillers Inc., United States
Hoochery Distillery, Australia
Huncol Ltd., Barbados
Inner Circle Rum Pty Ltd., Australia
J.A.J. Sprock Inc., Curacao
John D. Taylor's Velvet Falernum, Barbados
Kimberly Rum Company, Australia
La Mauny, Martinique
Laird and Company, United States
Longueteau, Guadeloupe
Malibu, Barbados and United States
Marimba Rum Company, United States

Martin Doorly & Co., Barbados
Matusalem & Co., United States
McCormick Distilling Co., Inc.
Montebello, Guadeloupe
Mount Gay Distilleries Ltd., Barbados
Musee Du Rhum, Guadeloupe
Panama Jack, United States
Paramount Distillers, United States
Pere Labat, Guadeloupe
Phillips Distilling Company, United States
PlayersExtreme.com, United States
Prichards' Distillery, United States
Pusser's West Indies, Ltd., British Virgin Islands
Rhum JM, Martinique
Rhum Saint-Maurice, French Guiana
Ron Zacapa Centenario, Guatemala
Smith Bowman Distillery, United States

100
RUM WEBSITES

http://www.10cane.com/
http://www.267.com/

http://www.admiralnelsonsrum.com
http://www.africanrum.com/
http://www.agualuca.com/
http://www.alnwickrum.com/
http://www.amrutwhisky.co.uk/index.php?f=data_home&a=2
http://www.angostura.com
http://www.antiguadistillery.com/
http://www.appletonrum.com/
http://www.avirtualdominica.com/rum.htm#mac

http://www.bacardi.com
http://www.bacardiflavors.com
http://www.bacardimojito.com/
http://www.bamburum.com/
http://www.barbancourt.net
http://www.bardenay.com
http://www.bartonbrands.com/bartongold.html
http://www.berniko.com/
http://www.bharatdistilleriesltd.com/Products.htm

http://www.bigblackdickrum.com/Rum.html
http://www.brinleygoldrum.com/
http://www.brugal.com/
http://www.bundabergrum.com.au

http://www.canefire.net/
http://www.canneroyale.com/
http://www.caribbean-spirits.com/Martinique.htm#lafavorite
http://www.castriescream.com
http://www.centenariointernacional.com
http://www.charbay.com/html/rum.html
http://www.ciclonrum.com/
http://www.cockspurrum.com/
http://www.cruzanrum.com/

http://www.danaimporters.com/danamain.html
http://www.demrum.com
http://www.donq.com/
http://www.doorlysrum.com/
http://www.dubar.com.do/

http://www.e8rum.com/
http://www.eldorado-rum.com/

http://www.flordecana.com/

http://www.goslingsrum.com/
http://www.greenislandrum.com/
http://www.grenadines.net/carriacou/jackiron.htm
http://www.guavaberry.com/guavaberry.htm

http://www.haleakaladistillers.com/
http://www.havana-club.com/
http://www.highwood-distillers.com/highwood.html
http://www.honeyrum.com/
http://www.hoochery.com.au/

http://www.innercirclerum.com/

http://www.kittlingridge.com/products.htm
http://www.khukrirum.com/

http://www.lairdandcompany.com/

http://www.malibu-rum.com/
http://www.mariebrizard.com/en/gamme,11,1,,la-mauny-rum.html
http://www.ministryofrum.com/
http://www.montecristorum.com/
http://www.mountgay.com/
http://www.mulatarum.ca/

http://www.neworleansrum.com/

http://www.oldmillrum.com/

http://www.phillipsdistilling.com/
http://www.plantationrum.com/en/index.php
http://www.playersextreme.com
http://www.pocotequila.com/mextour/ron.porfidio.html
http://www.prichardsdistillery.com
http://www.probrandsinc.com/
http://www.puertoricorums.com/
http://www.pussers.com/

http://www.raggedrockrum.com/en/index
http://www.redpiraterum.com/
http://www.redrum.com/
http://www.rhumdemartinique.com/duquesne/index_en.asp
http://www.rumjumbie.com/
http://www.ronbermudez.com/
http://www.ronzacapacentenario.com/
http://www.rum.co.uk/
http://www.rumcapital.com/

http://www.rumpunch.co.uk/
http://www.rumstory.co.uk/shop.shtml
http://www.rumuniversity.com/

http://www.santiagodecuba.co.uk
http://www.screechrum.com/
http://www.seawynderum.com
http://www.seventiki.co.nz/
http://www.shangorum.com/
http://www.shaw-ross.com
http://www.sikkimdistilleries.com/rums.htm
http://www.star-indust.com/
http://www.stock-austria.at/
http://www.stroh.at/anim1.html
http://www.sunsetrum.com/

http://www.tanduay.com
http://www.tommybahamarum.com/
http://www.tortugarums.com
http://www.turnercom.net/demarera/home.html

http://www.whalersrum.com/
http://www.woodsrum.co.uk/
http://www.worthyparkestate.com/bulkrum.html

GLOSSARY

TOOLS YOU WILL NEED:

Bar spoon: A long spoon for stirring cocktails or pitchers.

Blender: For blending drinks or crushing ice. Remember to save your blade by always pouring in the liquid before the ice.

Cocktail shaker and mixing/measuring glass: There are countless designs to choose from, but the standard is the Boston. It's a mixing glass that fits snugly into a stainless steel cone.

Ice bag: To crush ice use a rubber mallet and a lint-free or canvas ice bag, often referred to as a Lewis ice bag.

Ice bucket: Should have a vacuum seal and the ability to hold three trays of ice.

Ice scoop/tongs/ice pick: Never use your hands to pick up ice; use a scoop or tongs. The ice pick can help you unstick ice or break it up.

Jigger/measuring glass: Made from glass or metal. All drinks should be made using these bar tools. Remember that drinks on the rocks and mixed drinks should contain no more than 2 oz. of alcohol.

Knife and cutting board: A sturdy board and a small, very sharp paring knife are essential for cutting fruit garnishes.

Muddler: Use this small wooden bat or pestle to crush fruit, herbs, or cracked ice. Muddlers come in all different sizes and are used for making Stixx drinks.

Napkins/coasters: To place a drink on, hold a drink with, and for basic convenience.

Pitcher of water: Keep it clean. Someone always wants water and you certainly will use it.

Pourer: A helpful way to pour directly into the glass. A lidded spout helps keep everything but the drink out.

Stirrers/straws: Use them to sip, stir, and mix drinks. Glass is preferred for the mixer/stirrer. They can be custom molded and come in all different shapes and colors. (See www.bradnedstirs.com/printabledrinkstirs.html for options.)

Strainer: The strainer, quite simply, prevents ice from pouring out of the shaker. The two most common types in use are the Hawthorne and the Julep. The Hawthorne, with its distinctive coil rim, is most often used when pouring from the metal part of the Boston shaker. The Julep is a perforated metal spoon-like strainer used when pouring from the glass part of the Boston.

Swizzle stick: A fancy stirrer, oftentimes with the establishment's name on it.

Wine/bottle opener: They come in all shapes and sizes; the best is the industry standard waiter's opener. It opens cans as well as snapping off bottle tops, and it has a sharp blade.

GLASSWARE

Brandy snifters: Smaller sizes of the glasses, which come in sizes ranging from 5½ to 22 oz., are perfect for serving cognac, liqueurs, and premium whiskeys. The larger sizes provide enough space for full aroma, and the small stems on large bowls allow a cupped hand to warm the liquid.

Champagne glass: A narrow version of the standard wine glass has a tapered bowl to prevent those tiny bubbles from escaping and is usually never more than half filled. Also preferable for any sparkling liquid, including ciders.

Cocktail or martini glass: Perfect for martinis and Manhattans; remember that the stem is not just for show—it keeps hands from warming the drink. Available in 3- to 6-oz. sizes.

Coolers: These large-capacity tumblers are taller and hold a lot of ice for larger concoctions. They have become popular as of late for non-alcoholic and extra-volume highballs.

Highball glass: Extremely versatile glass available in many sizes and used for almost any drink. Usually clear and tall, the most popular sizes range from 8 to 12 oz.

Hurricane glass: Tropical fruit drinks and Bloody Marys are perfectly suited for these 16- to 23-oz. tall, curved glasses.

Rocks glasses: These "old-fashioned" glasses hold from 6 to 10 oz. and are used for on-the-rocks presentations. Double rocks will run between 12 and 15 oz.

Shot glass: The old standby can also be used as a measuring glass and is a must for every bar.

MIXING TERMS:

Build: In a glass full of ice, first pour in the liquor or spirit, then add the mixer. Add stirring/swizzle stick to stir the cocktail.

Fill: After you add ice and liquor or spirits, fill with mixer to within ¼ inch of the top.

Floating: To layer one ingredient on the top of a shot or cocktail.

Layering: Topping one ingredient over another.

TYPES OF DRINKS

Apertif: A light alcohol drink served before lunch or dinner; sometimes bitter.

Blended drinks: Blender drinks consisting of ice, ice cream, and a variety of other ingredients blended to a smooth and thick consistency.

Cobbler: A tall drink usually filled with crushed ice and garnished with fruit or mint.

Cream: Any drink made with ice cream, heavy cream, half-and-half, or any of the famous bottled cream drinks.

Crusta: Served in a wine glass with sugar-coated rim and the inside of the glass lined with a citrus rind.

Cups: A traditionally British category of wine-based drinks.

Daisy: An oversized cocktail sweetened with fruit syrup served over crushed ice.

Eggnog: A blend of milk or cream, beaten eggs, sugar, and liquor, usually rum, brandy, whiskey, and sometimes sherry, topped with nutmeg.

Flip: Cold, creamy drinks made with eggs, sugar, alcohol, and citrus juice.

Highball: A tall drink usually served with whiskey and ginger ale. The favorite drink of many drinkers' grandparents.

Grog: A rum-based drink made with fruit and sugar.

Julep: A tall sweet drink usually made with bourbon, water, sugar, crushed ice, and, occasionally, mint. The most popular julep is, of course, the Kentucky Derby's famous mint julep.

Mist: Any type of alcoholic beverage served over crushed ice.

Mojito: A Cuban-born drink prepared with sugar, muddled mint leaves, fresh lime juice, rum, ice, and soda water, garnished with mint leaves.

Puff: Made with equal parts alcohol and milk topped with club soda.

Pousse-Café: A drink made with layers created by floating liqueurs according to their density.

Rickey: A cocktail made of alcohol (usually whiskey, lime juice, and soda water).

Shooter: A straight shot of alcohol; also sometimes called serving a drink "neat."

Sling: A tall drink made with lemon juice and sugar and topped with club soda.

Sours: Drinks made with lemon juice, sugar, and alcohol.

Stixx: Tall muddled cocktails using different sized muddlers from 6 inches to 12 inches. Now they are muddling herbs, fruits, spices, and a variety of ethnic and regional ingredients, including beans, roots, and spices.

Toddy: Served hot, it's a mixture of alcohol, spices, and hot water.

Toppers: Blended drinks with ice cream or crushed ice—the thicker the better, which is why these drinks are served with a spoon and a straw. They are made using cordials, flavored rums, flavored vodkas, blended fresh fruits, and tropical juices. They are topped with crushed candy, fruits, nuts, and just about anything you can eat with a spoon.

HOW TO RIM YOUR GLASS:

Coating the rim of a glass with salt, sugar, or any other substance adds a decorative touch that improves the presentation of the cocktail.

Simple steps:

Moisten the rim of the glass (a lime wedge to rim a margarita, water or liqueur to sugar-rim for Kahlúa or chocolate martini).

Dip the rim in whatever ingredient you want to coat the glass with.

Slowly turn the glass to ensure you coat evenly.

Shake off any excess

Fill the glass with your prepared cocktail.

For more information and different cocktail rimmers, go to www.stirrings.com.

INDEX

B

Italian Colada, 124

Pork Chops with Pineapple
    Sauce, 263
Port Royal, 196
Presidente, 196
Prichards' Crystal rum, 84, 94
Prichards' Fine Tennessee rum, 225
Princess Morgan, 197
Professor & Mary Anne, 197
Puerto Rican dark rum, 41, 52, 61,
    85, 123, 197, 200, 212, 260, 270
Puerto Rican golden rum, 87, 116
Puerto Rican light rum, 49, 50, 52,
    90, 104, 184, 189, 200, 236, 248,
    250, 252, 253, 255, 265, 266,
    269, 270, 274
Puerto Rican rum, 211, 245, 257,
    258, 266, 272
Puerto Rican Rum Cappuccino, 197
Puerto Rican white rum, 45, 46,
    63, 92, 107, 124, 125, 156, 196
Pumpkin Spice, 198
Punch Islands, 198
Purple Dew, 198
Purple Flirt, 199
Pusser's rum, 132, 186
Pyrat Cask 23 rum, 200
Pyrat Punch, 199
Pyrat's Sin, 200
Pyrat Superior Blanco rum, 65
Pyrat XO Refresher, 199
Pyrat XO Reserve rum, 21, 49, 64,
    72, 76, 89, 109, 118, 168, 170,
    199, 227

Q

Quarter Deck, 200
Queens Park Swizzle, 200

R

Racer's Edge, 201
Raspberry Colada, 201
Raspberry Frost, 202
Raspberry Lemonade, 202
R & B, 201
Red Hawaiian, 202
Red Hot Mama, 203
Red Rhumba, 203
RedRum, 48, 52, 96, 110, 124, 127,
    130, 202, 203, 204, 225, 231
RedRum on the Beach, 203
RedRum Tsunami, 204
Red Velvet Vice, 204
Reggae Punch, 204
Reserve Mai Tai, 205
Rhum Barbancourt, 56, 66, 77,
    104, 105, 194, 207, 217
Rhum Barbancourt, white, 7, 100,
    198
Rhum Barbancourt 3 Stars, 42, 193
Rhum de Martinique, dark, 195
Rhum de Martinique, white, 82,
    195
Ricco, 205
Riki Tiki, 205
Roast Turkey with Stuffing, 263
Ron Anejo Pampero Especial
    rum, 169
Roots 'N' Culture, 206

Ray Foley, a former Marine with over thirty years of bartending and restaurant experience, is the founder and publisher of *Bartender Magazine*. *Bartender Magazine* is the only magazine in the world specifically geared toward bartenders, and is one of the very few primarily designed for servers of alcohol. *Bartender Magazine* is enjoying its twenty-ninth year. It currently has a circulation of over 148,000 and is steadily growing.

After serving in the United States Marine Corps and attending Seton Hall University, Ray entered the restaurant business as a bartender, which eventually led to his position as Assistant General Manager of The Manor in West Orange, New Jersey, where he managed over 350 employees.

In 1983, Ray left The Manor to devote his full efforts to *Bartender Magazine*. The circulation and exposure has grown from seven thousand to over 148,000 to date and has become the largest on-premise liquor magazine in the country.

Ray has been published in numerous articles throughout the country and has appeared on TV and radio shows.
He is also the founder of the Bartender Hall of Fame™, which honors

the best bartenders throughout the United States not only for their abilities as bartenders, but for involvement in their communities as well.

In addition, Ray is the founder of the Bartenders' Foundation Incorporated™. This nonprofit foundation raises scholarship money for bartenders and their families. Scholarships awarded to bartenders can be used to further either their education or the education of their children.

Mr. Foley serves as a consultant to some of our nation's foremost distillers and importers. He is also responsible for naming and inventing new drinks for the liquor industry, including the Fuzzy Navel, the Royal Stretch, S.O.B, and the Royal Turf.

Ray has one of the largest collections of cocktail recipe books in the world, dating back to the 1800s. He is one of the foremost collectors of cocktail shakers, with over four hundred shakers in his collection.

Ray is also the author of: *The Ultimate Cocktail Book, The Ultimate Little Shooter Book, The Ultimate Little Martini Book, The Ultimate Little Frozen Drink Book, Advice from Anonymous, Spirits of Ireland, Beer Is the Answer . . . I Don't Remember the Question, X-Rated Drink Book, Bartending for Dummies, How to Run a Bar for Dummies,* Bartender Magazine's *Ultimate Bartender's Guide, The Vodka 1000,* and *The Tequila 1000.*

Ray resides in New Jersey with his wife and partner of twenty-five years, Jackie, and their son, Ryan. He is also the father of three other wonderful and bright children: Raymond Pindar, William, and Amy.

Ray is foremost and always will be a bartender.

For more information, please contact Jackie Foley at *Bartender Magazine,* PO Box 158, Liberty Corner, NJ 07938. Telephone: (908) 766–6006; FAX: (908) 766–6607; email: barmag@aol.com; website: www.bartender.com.